PRACTICE – ASSESS – D

# 180 Days of WRITING
## for Second Grade

- Prewriting
- Drafting
- Revising
- Editing
- Publishing

**Author**

Brenda A. Van Dixhorn

Shell Education

### Standards

For information on how this resource meets national and other state standards, see pages 4–6. You may also review this information by scanning the QR code or visiting our website at http://www.shelleducation.com and following the on-screen directions.

## Publishing Credits

Corinne Burton, M.A.Ed., *President*; Emily R. Smith, M.A.Ed., *Content Director*; Jennifer Wilson, *Editor*; Grace Alba Le, *Multimedia Designer*; Don Tran, *Production Artist*; Stephanie Bernard, *Assistant Editor*; Amber Goff, *Editorial Assistant*

## Image Credits

pp. 45, 62, 65, 89, 101, 105, 183–184, iStock; All other images Shutterstock.

## Standards

## Shell Education

5482 Argosy Avenue
Huntington Beach, CA  92649-1030
www.tcmpub.com/shell-education

**ISBN 978-1-4258-1525-7**

© 2020 Shell Education Publishing, Inc.

# TABLE OF CONTENTS

# INTRODUCTION

## The Need for Practice

To be successful in today's writing classrooms, students must deeply understand both concepts and procedures so that they can discuss and demonstrate their understanding. Demonstrating understanding is a process that must be continually practiced for students to be successful. Practice is especially important to help students apply their concrete, conceptual understanding of each particular writing skill.

## Understanding Assessment

In addition to providing opportunities for frequent practice, teachers must be able to assess students' writing skills. This is important so that teachers can adequately address students' misconceptions, build on their current understandings, and challenge them appropriately. Assessment is a long-term process that involves careful analysis of student responses from a discussion, project, practice sheet, or test. When analyzing the data, it is important for teachers to reflect on how their teaching practices may have influenced students' responses and to identify those areas where additional instruction may be required. In short, the data gathered from assessments should be used to inform instruction: slow down, speed up, or reteach. This type of assessment is called *formative assessment*.

# HOW TO USE THIS BOOK

With *180 Days of Writing*, creative, theme-based units guide students as they practice the five steps of the writing process: prewriting, drafting, revising, editing, and publishing. During each odd week (Weeks 1, 3, 5, etc.), students interact with mentor texts. Then, students apply their learning by writing their own pieces during each following even week (Weeks 2, 4, 6, etc.). Many practice pages also focus on grammar/language standards to help improve students' writing.

## Easy to Use and Standards Based

These daily activities reinforce grade-level skills across the various genres of writing: opinion, informative/explanatory, and narrative. Each day provides a full practice page, making the activities easy to prepare and implement as part of a classroom morning routine, at the beginning of each writing lesson, or as homework.

The chart below indicates the writing and language standards that are addressed throughout this book. See pages 5–6 for a breakdown of which writing standard is covered in each week. **Note:** Students may not have deep understandings of some topics in this book. Remember to assess students based on their writing skills and not their content knowledge.

## College and Career Readiness Standards

| |
|---|
| **Writing 2.1**—Write opinion pieces in which they introduce the topic they are writing about, state an opinion, support the opinion, and provide a concluding statement. |
| **Writing 2.2**—Write informative/explanatory texts in which they introduce a topic, use facts and definitions to develop points, and provide a concluding statement or section. |
| **Writing 2.3**—Write narratives in which they recount a well-elaborated event or short sequence of events. |
| **Language 2.1**—Demonstrate the command of the conventions of standard English grammar and usage when writing or speaking. |
| **Language 2.2**—Demonstrate command of the conventions of standard English capitalization, punctuation, and spelling when writing. |
| **Language 2.5**—Demonstrate understanding of word relationships and nuances in word meanings. |

# HOW TO USE THIS BOOK (cont.)

Below is a list of overarching themes, corresponding weekly themes, and the writing standards that students will encounter throughout this book.  For each overarching theme, students will interact with mentor texts in the odd week and then apply their learning by writing their own pieces in the even week.  **Note:** The writing prompt for each week can be found on pages 7–8.  You may wish to display the prompts in the classroom for students to reference throughout the appropriate weeks.

| Overarching Themes | Weekly Themes | Standards |
|---|---|---|
| Ready to Learn | **Week 1:** Rules for School<br>**Week 2:** Friends at School | **Writing 2.3**—Write narratives in which they recount a well-elaborated event or short sequence of events. |
| Where People Live | **Week 3:** In the City<br>**Week 4:** In the Country | **Writing 2.2**—Write informative/explanatory texts in which they introduce a topic, use facts and definitions to develop points, and provide a concluding statement or section. |
| Fall Fruit | **Week 5:** Why Eat Apples<br>**Week 6:** How to Eat Apples | **Writing 2.1**—Write opinion pieces in which they introduce the topic they are writing about, state an opinion, support the opinion, and provide a concluding statement. |
| A Walk in the Woods | **Week 7:** Rainforests<br>**Week 8:** Temperate Forests | **Writing 2.2**—Write informative/explanatory texts in which they introduce a topic, use facts and definitions to develop points, and provide a concluding statement or section. |
| Are They Scary? | **Week 9:** Jack-o-Lanterns<br>**Week 10:** Scarecrows | **Writing 2.1**—Write opinion pieces in which they introduce the topic they are writing about, state an opinion, support the opinion, and provide a concluding statement. |
| Thankfulness | **Week 11:** Being Thankful<br>**Week 12:** Sharing Thanks | **Writing 2.1**—Write opinion pieces in which they introduce the topic they are writing about, state an opinion, support the opinion, and provide a concluding statement. |
| Weird Weather | **Week 13:** Thunderstorms<br>**Week 14:** Snowstorms | **Writing 2.2**—Write informative/explanatory texts in which they introduce a topic, use facts and definitions to develop points, and provide a concluding statement or section. |
| Time to Give | **Week 15:** Gifts to Me<br>**Week 16:** Giving to Others | **Writing 2.3**—Write narratives in which they recount a well-elaborated event or short sequence of events. |
| Staying Warm | **Week 17:** Building Snowmen<br>**Week 18:** Sledding | **Writing 2.3**—Write narratives in which they recount a well-elaborated event or short sequence of events. |
| Black and White | **Week 19:** Zebras<br>**Week 20:** Penguins | **Writing 2.2**—Write informative/explanatory texts in which they introduce a topic, use facts and definitions to develop points, and provide a concluding statement or section. |
| Our Country | **Week 21:** Important People<br>**Week 22:** Important Places | **Writing 2.1**—Write opinion pieces in which they introduce the topic they are writing about, state an opinion, support the opinion and provide a concluding statement. |

# HOW TO USE THIS BOOK *(cont.)*

| Overarching Themes | Weekly Themes | Standards |
|---|---|---|
| In the Present | **Week 23:** Little Red Riding Hood <br> **Week 24:** Goldilocks and the Three Bears | **Writing 2.3**—Write narratives in which they recount a well-elaborated event or short sequence of events. |
| Looking Green | **Week 25:** Frogs <br> **Week 26:** Turtles | **Writing 2.2**—Write informative/explanatory texts in which they introduce a topic, use facts and definitions to develop points, and provide a concluding statement or section. |
| Out in Space | **Week 27:** Planets <br> **Week 28:** Sun, Moon, and Stars | **Writing 2.3**—Write narratives in which they recount a well-elaborated event or short sequence of events. |
| Just a Day | **Week 29:** A Great Day <br> **Week 30:** A Bad Day | **Writing 2.3**—Write narratives in which they recount a well-elaborated event or short sequence of events. |
| Picnic Pests | **Week 31:** Ants <br> **Week 32:** Bees | **Writing 2.1**—Write opinion pieces in which they introduce the topic they are writing about, state an opinion, support the opinion, and provide a concluding statement. |
| Movement | **Week 33:** In the Wind <br> **Week 34:** Push or Pull | **Writing 2.2**—Write informative/explanatory texts in which they introduce a topic, use facts and definitions to develop points, and provide a concluding statement or section. |
| Free Time | **Week 35:** Watching TV or Reading? <br> **Week 36:** Beach or Park? | **Writing 2.1**—Write opinion pieces in which they introduce the topic they are writing about, state an opinion, support the opinion, and provide a concluding statement. |

## Weekly Setup

Write each prompt on the board throughout the appropriate week. Students should reference the prompts as they work through the activity pages so that they stay focused on the topics and the right genre of writing: opinion, informative/explanatory, and narrative. You may wish to print copies of this chart from the digital resources (filename: G2_writingprompts.pdf) and distribute them to students to keep throughout the school year.

| Week | Prompt |
|---|---|
| 1 | Many schools have rules that students should follow. Describe a time where your class set up rules for the classroom. |
| 2 | Describe a time when you have played with a friend at school. |
| 3 | Think about the city. Describe what it looks like and what happens there. |
| 4 | Describe what a countryside looks like and what happens there. |
| 5 | There are many reasons why people should eat apples. Describe why people should eat apples. Include reasons to support your opinion. |
| 6 | Describe the best way to eat apples. Include reasons to support your opinion. |
| 7 | Describe a rainforest. Include details about how the forest looks and smells. |
| 8 | Describe a temperate forest. Include details about how the forest looks and smells. |
| 9 | Do you think jack-o-lanterns are scary? Write a paragraph stating your opinion and details to help support your opinion. |
| 10 | Do you think scarecrows are scary? Write a paragraph stating your opinion. Add details to help support your opinion. |
| 11 | What is the best way to be thanked by someone? Explain why it is the best way. |

| Week | Prompt |
|---|---|
| 12 | What is the best way to give thanks to someone? Explain why it is the best way. |
| 13 | Describe what a thunderstorm is. Include details about what it looks like and the dangers it can cause. |
| 14 | Describe what a snowstorm is. Include details about what it looks like and the dangers it can cause. |
| 15 | Think about a time you received a gift. Write a narrative about what the gift was, who gave it to you, and what the gift means to you. |
| 16 | Think about a time you gave someone a gift. Write a narrative about what the gift was, how you picked it out, and how the person reacted when they opened it. |
| 17 | Describe a time you have either built a snowman or what you think building a snowman might be like. Include details about the day. |
| 18 | Describe a time you have either gone sledding or what you think sledding might be like. Include details about the day. |
| 19 | Write a paragraph about zebras. Include facts about where they live and their physical characteristics. |
| 20 | Write a paragraph about penguins. Include facts about where they live and their physical characteristics. |

# HOW TO USE THIS BOOK *(cont.)*

| Week | Prompt |
|---|---|
| 21 | Write a paragraph about important people. Include details explaining why they are important. |
| 22 | Write a paragraph about a place that is important to you. Include details such as where it is located. |
| 23 | Write a modern version of *Little Red Riding Hood*. Include dialogue and a strong conclusion. |
| 24 | Write a modern version of *Goldilocks and the Three Bears*. Include dialogue and a strong conclusion. |
| 25 | Explain what frogs look like. Provide descriptive details using various adjectives. |
| 26 | Explain what turtles look like. Provide descriptive details using various adjectives. |
| 27 | Imagine you are on a trip in outer space. Write a narrative about the different planets you see on your adventure. |
| 28 | Imagine you are on a trip through outer space. Write a narrative about what you see and do on your adventure. |
| 29 | Have you ever had a great day? Describe what happened and what you did. |
| 30 | Have you ever had a bad day? Describe what happened and what you did to make the day better. |
| 31 | Do you think ants are useful? Explain your answer and give supporting details. |
| 32 | Do you think bees are useful? Explain your answer and give supporting details. |

| Week | Prompt |
|---|---|
| 33 | Describe how objects are affected by the wind. Include and describe types of objects that can and cannot be blown over by the wind. |
| 34 | Describe how objects are pushed or pulled. Include the differences between pulling and pushing. |
| 35 | Do you prefer watching television or reading? Explain why using strong supporting details. |
| 36 | Do you prefer the beach or the park? Explain why using strong supporting details. |

#51525—180 Days of Writing

# HOW TO USE THIS BOOK *(cont.)*

## Using the Practice Pages

The activity pages provide practice and assessment opportunities for each day of the school year. Teachers may wish to prepare packets of weekly practice pages for the classroom or for homework. As outlined on pages 5–6, each two-week unit is aligned to one writing standard. **Note:** Before implementing each week's activity pages, review the corresponding prompt on pages 7–8 with students and have students brainstorm thoughts about each topic.

On odd weeks, students practice the daily skills using mentor texts. On even weeks, students use what they have learned in the previous week and apply it to their own writing.

Each day focuses on one of the steps in the writing process: prewriting, drafting, revising, editing, and publishing.

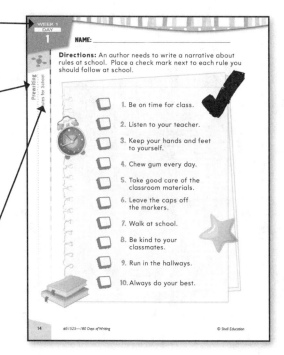

There are 18 overarching themes. Each odd week and the following even week focus on unique themes that fit under one overarching theme. For a list of the overarching themes and individual weekly themes, see pages 5–6.

## Using the Resources

The following resources will be helpful to students as they complete the activity pages. Print copies of these resources and provide them to students to keep at their desks.

Rubrics for the three genres of writing (opinion, informative/explanatory, and narrative) can be found on pages 202–204. Use the rubrics to assess students' writing at the end of each even week. Be sure to share these rubrics with students often so that they know what is expected of them.

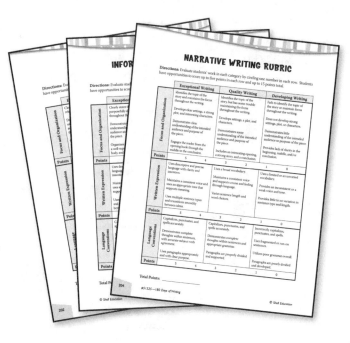

# HOW TO USE THIS BOOK *(cont.)*

## Using the Resources *(cont.)*

*The Writing Process* can be found on page 208 and in the digital resources (filename: G2_writing_process.pdf). Students can reference each step of the writing process as they move through each week.

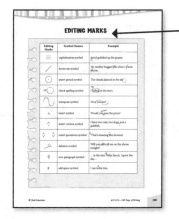

*Editing Marks* can be found on page 209 and in the digital resources (filename: G2_editing_marks.pdf). Students may need to reference this page as they work on the editing activities (Day 4s).

If you wish to have students peer or self-edit their writing, a *Peer/Self-Editing Checklist* is provided in the digital resources (filename: G2_peer_checklist.pdf).

*Writing Signs* for each of the writing genres are on pages 213–215 and in the digital resources (filename: G2_writing_signs.pdf). Hang the signs up during the appropriate two-week units to remind students which type of writing they are focusing on.

*Writing Tips* pages for each of the writing genres can be found on pages 210–212 and in the digital resources (filename: G2_writing_tips.pdf). Students can reference the appropriate *Writing Tips* pages as they work through the weeks.

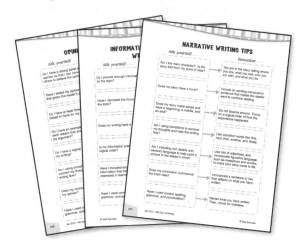

# HOW TO USE THIS BOOK *(cont.)*

## Diagnostic Assessment

Teachers can use the practice pages as diagnostic assessments. The data analysis tools included with the book enable teachers or parents to quickly score students' work and monitor their progress. Teachers and parents can quickly see which writing skills students may need to target further to develop proficiency.

After students complete each two-week unit, score each students' even week Day 5 published piece using the appropriate, genre-specific rubric (pages 202–204). Then, complete the *Practice Page Item Analysis* (pages 205–207) that matches the writing genre. These charts are also provided in the digital resources (filenames: G2_opinion_analysis.pdf, G2_informative_analysis.pdf, G2_narrative_analysis.pdf). Teachers can input data into the electronic files directly on the computer, or they can print the pages and analyze students' work using paper and pencil.

## To Complete the Practice Page Item Analyses:

- Write or type students' names in the far-left column. Depending on the number of students, more than one copy of the form may be needed or you may need to add rows.

- The weeks in which the particular writing genres are the focus are indicated across the tops of the charts. **Note:** Students are only assessed on the even weeks, therefore the odd weeks are not included on the charts.

- For each student, record his or her rubric score in the appropriate column.

- Add the scores for each student after they've focused on a particular writing genre twice. Place that sum in the far right column. Use these scores as benchmarks to determine how each student is performing. This allows for three benchmarks during the year that you can use to gather formative diagnostic data.

# HOW TO USE THIS BOOK *(cont.)*

## Using the Results to Differentiate Instruction

Once results are gathered and analyzed, teachers can use the results to inform the way they differentiate instruction. The data can help determine which writing types are the most difficult for students and which students need additional instructional support and continued practice.

### Whole-Class Support

The results of the diagnostic analysis may show that the entire class is struggling with a particular writing genre. If these concepts have been taught in the past, this indicates that further instruction or reteaching is necessary. If these concepts have not been taught in the past, this data is a great preassessment and may demonstrate that students do not have a working knowledge of the concepts. Thus, careful planning for the length of the unit(s) or lesson(s) must be considered, and additional front-loading may be required.

### Small-Group or Individual Support

The results of the diagnostic analysis may show that an individual student or a small group of students is struggling with a particular writing genre. If these concepts have been taught in the past, this indicates that further instruction or reteaching is necessary. Consider pulling these students aside to instruct them further on the concept(s), while others are working independently. Students may also benefit from extra practice using games or computer-based resources. Teachers can also use the results to help identify individual students or groups of proficient students who are ready for enrichment or above-grade-level instruction. These students may benefit from independent learning contracts or more challenging activities.

## Digital Resources

Reference page 216 for information about accessing the digital resources and an overview of the contents.

# STANDARDS CORRELATIONS

Shell Education is committed to producing educational materials that are research and standards based. In this effort, we have correlated all of our products to the academic standards of all 50 states, the District of Columbia, the Department of Defense Dependents Schools, and all Canadian provinces.

## How to Find Standards Correlations

To print a customized correlation report of this product for your state, visit our website at **www.tcmpub.com/shell-education** and follow the on-screen directions. If you require assistance in printing correlation reports, please contact our Customer Service Department at 1-877-777-3450.

## Purpose and Intent of Standards

Legislation mandates that all states adopt academic standards that identify the skills students will learn in kindergarten through grade twelve. Many states also have standards for Pre-K. This same legislation sets requirements to ensure the standards are detailed and comprehensive.

Standards are designed to focus instruction and guide adoption of curricula. Standards are statements that describe the criteria necessary for students to meet specific academic goals. They define the knowledge, skills, and content students should acquire at each level. Standards are also used to develop standardized tests to evaluate students' academic progress.

Teachers are required to demonstrate how their lessons meet state standards. State standards are used in the development of all of our products, so educators can be assured they meet the academic requirements of each state.

The activities in this book are aligned to today's national and state-specific college and career readiness standards. The chart on page 4 lists the writing and language standards used throughout this book. A more detailed chart on pages 5–6 correlates the specific writing standards to each week.

Prewriting
Rules for School

NAME: _____

**Directions:** An author needs to write a narrative about rules at school. Place a check mark next to each rule the author should include.

☐ 1. Be on time for class.

☐ 2. Listen to your teacher.

☐ 3. Keep your hands and feet to yourself.

☐ 4. Chew gum every day.

☐ 5. Take good care of the classroom materials.

☐ 6. Leave the caps off the markers.

☐ 7. Walk at school.

☐ 8. Be kind to your classmates.

☐ 9. Run in the hallways.

☐ 10. Always do your best.

NAME: _____

**Directions:** Read the narrative paragraph.  Underline the steps that the class takes in setting rules for the classroom.

It was a great first day of school.  I am in second grade at Elliott Grove Elementary School.  My teacher is Mrs. Wright.  Today, our class decided we should have class rules that we would all follow.  Mrs. Wright gave each of us three sheets of paper and asked us to write a classroom rule on each one.  Our class looked at the rules we had written and found many that were the same.  We chose five rules for our class to follow this year.  I know it is going to be a good year!

# Printing Practice abc

**Directions:** Use your best printing to write a sentence about one rule you follow at school.

_____

_____

NAME: _____

**Directions:** Read the paragraph. The sentences in the middle are out of order. Write the numbers 1, 2, and 3 to put them in the correct order.

Every classroom needs rules. _____Then, we think about which rules we should have. _____Finally, we follow the rules we create. _____First, we decide we should have rules. This way, our classroom will be a safe environment.

## Boost Your Learning! 🚀

**Sequence words** help the reader know when things happen in a story. Add these words to your writing to help make it clear for the reader.

NAME: _____

**Directions:** Use the ☰ symbol to correct the words that should be capitalized.

1. My sister attends abraham lincoln Preschool and has to follow the rules.

2. Our teacher, mrs. gillespie, has worked hard to set up rules at park heights school.

3. mr. Bolander allows his class to set up their own classroom rules.

4. mrs. Eddy reminds her students how helpful rules can be.

## Boost Your Learning! 🚀

Specific names of people and places should be capitalized in your writing.

**Example:** mrs. weldin teaches at springs elementary school.

NAME: _____

**Directions:** Revisit the narrative paragraph. Circle the words that are capitalized correctly. Underline the sequence words. Then, answer the question.

It was a great first day of school. I am in second grade at Elliott Grove Elementary School. My teacher is Mrs. Wright. Today, our class decided we should have class rules that we would all follow. Then, Mrs. Wright gave each of us three sheets of paper and asked us to write a classroom rule on each one. Our class looked at the rules we had written and found many that were the same. We chose five rules for our class to follow this year. I know it is going to be a good year!

**1.** What makes the paragraph above a strong narrative?

_____

_____

_____

**This week I learned:** ✏️

- to capitalize the names of specific people and places
- to use sequence words to help tell a story

**NAME:** _____

**Directions:** Think of three friends you have at school. Write the name of each friend. Then, list one thing you do with each friend at school.

**My friend is:** _____

**Things I have done with my friend:** _____

_____

_____

_____

**My friend is:** _____

**Things I have done with my friend:** _____

_____

_____

_____

**My friend is:** _____

**Things I have done with my friend:** _____

_____

_____

_____

Drafting
Friends at School

NAME: _____

**Directions:** Describe a time when you have played with a friend at school.  Use your notes from page 19 to help you.

_____

_____

_____

_____

_____

_____

_____

_____

_____

_____

_____

_____

_____

**Remember!**

A strong narrative includes:

- an introductory sentence

- sentences that describe the events

- names of specific people and places

## Printing Practice  abc

**Directions:** Use your best printing to write two adjectives about your friend.

_____

_____

**NAME:** _____

**Directions:** Circle the words that you like to use to help a reader understand the sequence of a story.

| | |
|---|---|
| then | next |
| before | after |
| earlier | second |
| first | last |
| third | later |
| finally | |

# Time to Improve!

**Directions:** Go back to the draft you wrote on page 20. Add sequence words to make it easier for the reader to know when things happened.

**Example:** <sup>First,</sup> ^ I played soccer with him.

**NAME:** _____

**Directions:** Use the ≡ symbol to show which words in the sentences below need to be capitalized.

1. It is fun to play with my friends amir, lily, and aisha.

2. We are all in second grade at fern hill elementary school.

3. My mom drives me to paul revere park to play with my friend, gabe.

4. ariel's little sister likes to play with us at the park, too.

# Time to Improve! 🎖

**Directions:** Go back to the draft you wrote on page 20. Look for words that need to be capitalized.

 #51525—180 Days of Writing

**NAME:** _____

**Directions:** Describe a time when you have played with a friend at school.

_____

_____

_____

_____

_____

_____

_____

_____

_____

NAME: _____

**Directions:** In each window of the building, write one thing that is found in a city. Two examples are provided.

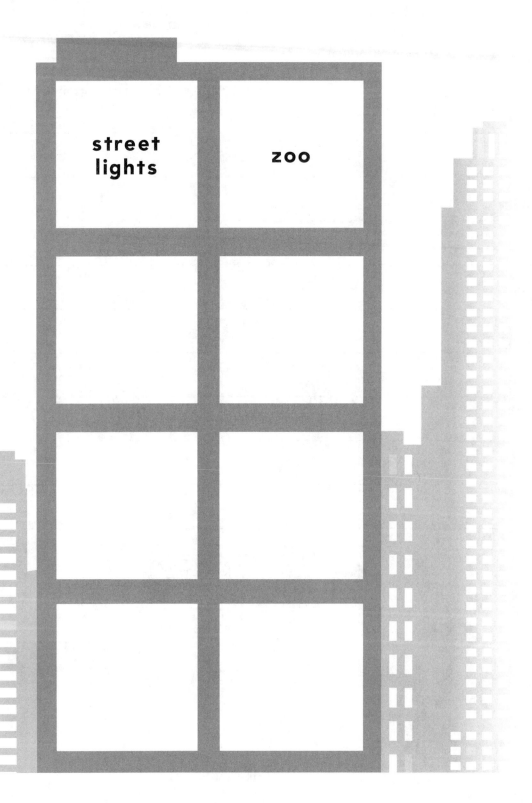

street lights

zoo

**NAME:** _____

**Directions:** Read the informative/explanatory paragraph. Underline the sentences that have facts in them. Then, answer the question.

The city is the best place to live. A city has parks where children can play. It is fun to go swimming. People can do many things in a city, such as go to a zoo or a museum. We have the best ball team in our city. Cities are busy places. Sometimes, the city can be too noisy. There is almost always something happening in a city.

## Printing Practice  abc

**Directions:** What do you think is fun to do in a city? Use your best printing to write your answer.

_____

_____

## Boost Your Learning! 🚀

Use facts to tell true information about a place you are describing.

**Revising**
In the City

**NAME:** _____

**Directions:** Write an adjective to describe each noun.

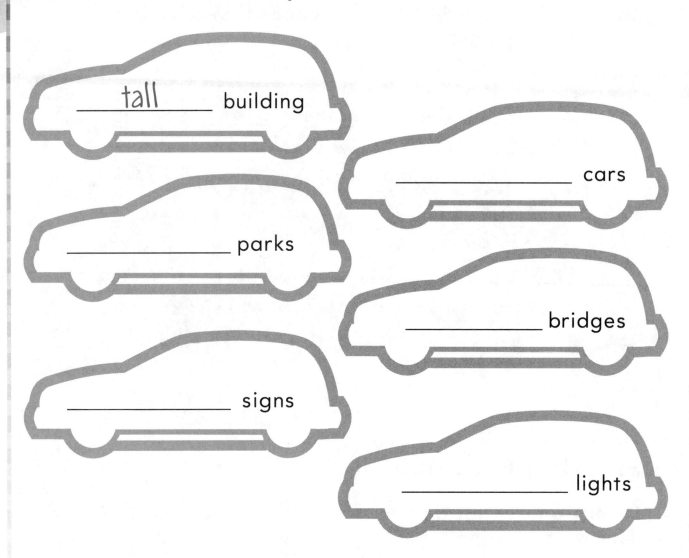

_____tall_____ building

_____ cars

_____ parks

_____ bridges

_____ signs

_____ lights

## Boost Your Learning!

**Adjectives** describe nouns. They tell what a person, place, or thing is like. Use adjectives to make your writing more interesting.

NAME: _____

**Directions:** Use the ∧ symbol to add adjectives in the sentences.

1. You can ride on buses in a city.

2. Some people like to go to the store.

3. There are many signs on city streets.

4. They have food in restaurants in many places.

5. Buses, trains, and taxis can help you get around in a city.

## Boost Your Learning! 🚀

Adjectives add details to your writing.

**Example:** When we went to the park, we
                                            ∧
swam in a pool with slides.      water
        ∧
     curvy

**NAME:** _____

**Directions:** Read the paragraph. Then, answer the question.

Many people live in the city. A city has big parks where children can play. It has large swimming pools, too. People can do many things in a city, such as go to a zoo or an interesting museum. Some cities have good baseball teams. Cities are busy places. Sometimes, the city can be noisy. There is almost always something happening in a city.

**1.** What makes this a strong paragraph?

_____

_____

_____

_____

_____

**This week I learned:**

- to use facts in informative/explanatory writing
- to add adjectives to make writing more interesting

**NAME:** _____

**Directions:** Put check marks in the cows with words that would be included in a paragraph about the countryside.

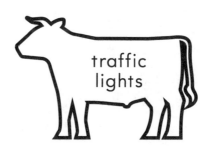

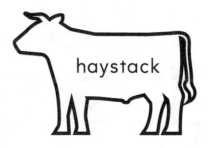

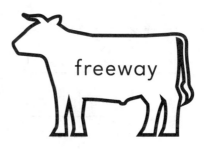

Drafting

In the Country

**NAME:** _____

**Directions:** Describe what a countryside looks like and what happens there. Use your choices from page 29 to help you.

_____

_____

_____

_____

_____

_____

_____

_____

_____

_____

_____

_____

**Remember!** 🔖

A strong informative/ explanatory paragraph includes:

- a topic sentence

- details to support the main idea

- a concluding sentence

## Printing Practice abc

**Directions:** What would you like to do in the countryside?

_____

NAME: _____

**Directions:** Add a noun after each adjective.

tall _____

high _____

pretty _____

smelly _____

soft _____

fuzzy _____

## Time to Improve!

**Directions:** Go back to the draft you wrote on page 30. Add adjectives to make it more interesting.

**Example:** There are flowers growing in the field.
                        ∧
              pink and yellow

Editing

In the Country

**NAME:** _____

**Directions:** Read the sentences. Add adjectives to the sentences to include more details. Rewrite the new detailed sentences on the lines.

1. The country is a place to live.

   _____

   _____

2. People take care of animals on farms.

   _____

   _____

3. There are not many people around in the country.

   _____

   _____

## Remember!

Add more details to your writing by including adjectives!

## Time to Improve!

**Directions:** Go back to the draft you wrote on page 30. Look for places where adjectives can be added to add more details.

**NAME:** _____

**Directions:** Describe what a countryside looks like and what happens there.

_____

_____

_____

_____

_____

_____

_____

_____

_____

_____

_____

**NAME:** _____

Prewriting

Why Eat Apples

**Directions:** Place check marks in the apples that explain why eating apples is good for you.

NAME: _____

**Directions:** Read the paragraph. Circle two times where the author states her opinion about eating apples. Then, underline each sentence that supports the opinion.

Everyone should eat apples every day. Apples are colorful and crunchy. Apples are healthy snacks. They have vitamins that help keep you from getting sick. Apples are delicious. Eating apples can make your heart strong. It is a good idea to eat an apple every day.

**Printing Practice** abc

**Directions:** Use your best printing to write one reason you should eat apples.

_____

_____

**NAME:** _____

**Directions:** Draw a line through each statement that does not support the opinion.

**Opinion: I prefer eating apples.**

There is an apple in my lunchbox.

I had a banana for breakfast.

**Opinion: The best thing about apples is that they are good for you.**

Apples come in many different colors.

Apples help make your heart strong.

**Opinion: I think apples make great snacks.**

My mom gave me crackers.

Apples are easy to carry and eat.

## Boost Your Learning! 🚀

Information that does not support the opinion sentence should be deleted. Show that you want to delete text by drawing a line through it.

**Example:** ~~Apples can be picked from trees in the fall.~~

NAME: _____

**Directions:** Write the nouns from the Noun Bank in the correct apples.

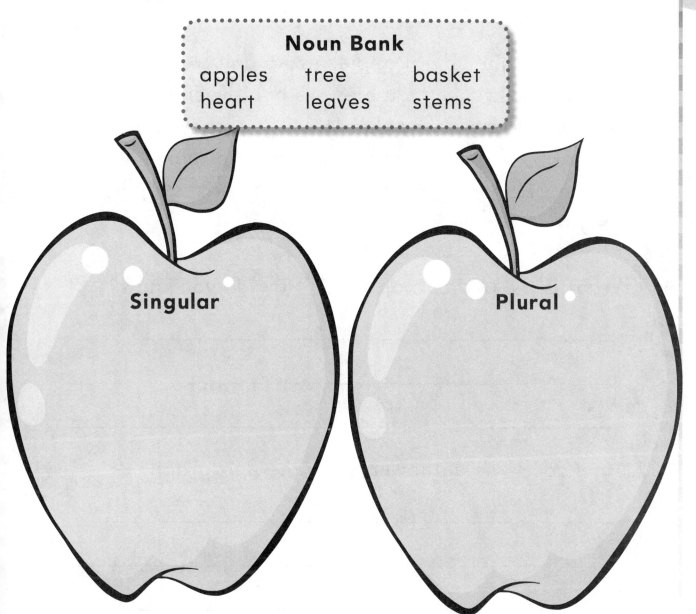

**Noun Bank**

| apples | tree | basket |
| heart | leaves | stems |

Singular

Plural

## Boost Your Learning!

Nouns that tell about more than one are called *plurals*. A **plural noun** can usually be formed by adding an *-s* or *-es* to the end of a word.

**NAME:** _____

**Directions:** Revisit the opinion paragraph. Then, answer the questions below.

Everyone should eat apples every day. Apples are colorful and crunchy. Apples are healthy snacks. They have vitamins that help keep you from getting sick. Apples are delicious. Eating apples can make your heart strong. It is a good idea to eat an apple every day.

**1.** What is the author's opinion? How do you know?

_____

_____

_____

**2.** How could the author improve the paragraph?

_____

_____

_____

**This week I learned:** 🖊✏️

- that sentences in a paragraph need to support the opinion sentence
- how to make nouns plural

**NAME:** _____

**Directions:** Circle your favorite way to eat apples in the middle apple. Then, write four reasons why you like eating apples that way in the outer apples.

I like eating apple slices.

I like eating apples with caramel sauce.

I like eating apple pie.

I like eating apple sauce.

**Drafting**

How to Eat Apples

**NAME:** _____

**Directions:** Describe the best way to eat apples.  Include reasons to support your opinion.  Use your notes on page 39 to help you.

_____

_____

_____

_____

_____

_____

_____

_____

_____

_____

_____

> ## Remember! 🖋
>
> A strong opinion paragraph includes:
>
> • an introductory sentence stating your opinion
>
> • support for your opinion
>
> • a concluding sentence

## Printing Practice  abc

**Directions:** Use your best printing to write two different ways to eat apples.

_____

_____

**NAME:** _____

**Directions:** Draw a line through each sentence that does not support the opinion sentence.

> The best way to enjoy apples is dipping them in caramel sauce. Apples are great snacks because there are so many ways they can be eaten. Each bite of a caramel apple is sweet and delicious. Do you like baked potatoes? I like when the caramel covers the entire apple. Apple pies, apple cake, and applesauce are good treats. Caramel apples are the best way to eat apples.

# Time to Improve! ⌛

**Directions:** Go back to the draft you wrote on page 40. Look for sentences that do not support your opinion sentence, and draw lines through them.

NAME: _____

**Directions:** Use the ∧ symbol to add an -s to each word to make it plural.

apple  pie  sauce  caramel

slice  cake  fruit

seed  core  stem  tree

## Time to Improve! 🏅

**Directions:** Revisit the draft you wrote on page 40. Look for nouns that need to be plural, and correct them.

**Example**: My favorite way to eat apple is to eat
                                              ∧
                                              s
them in pie.

**NAME:** _____

**Directions:** Describe the best way to eat apples. Include reasons to support your opinion.

**NAME:** _____

**Directions:** Draw an *X* on each leaf that does not belong in a rainforest.

trees

snakes

vines

swimming pools

dirt paths

grocery stores

leopards

birds

school buses

tree frogs

huts

libraries

apartment buildings

flowers

monkeys

#51525—180 Days of Writing

**NAME:** _____

**Drafting**
Rainforests

**Directions:** Read the informative/explanatory paragraph. Underline the topic sentence. Then, draft a concluding sentence that matches the topic sentence.

A rainforest is a feast for your senses. There are lots of plants, trees, and animals to see in rainforests. The flowers in rainforests have many smells. You can hear many noises that are made by the birds and other animals. Some plants feel smooth, while others feel quite bumpy. Some of the foods we taste, such as bananas, spices, and sugar, were first found in rainforests.

_____

_____

_____

_____

_____

## Printing Practice abc

**Directions:** Use your best printing to write two items that you would see in a rainforest.

_____     _____

Revising
Rainforests

**NAME:** _____

**Directions:** Read the sentences. The underlined words are repeated and should be replaced. Write synonyms on the lines to replace them.

1. You can see many plants in a rainforest, and you can <u>see</u> many animals.

   _____

2. People can hear birds flying, and people can <u>hear</u> the wind blowing in the trees.

   _____

3. There is a damp smell in the rainforest, and there is a <u>smell</u> of flowers, too.

   _____

## Boost Your Learning! 🚀

**Synonyms** are words that are the same or similar in meaning. Rather than using the same word over and over, use synonyms to make your writing more interesting!

NAME: _____

**Directions:** Read the paragraph.  Then, circle the misspelled words.  Write the correct spelling on the lines below.  **Hint:** There are six spelling errors.

Many diferent plants and animols make their homes in rainforrests.  Some trees grow viry tall, and other plants are closer to the grond.  Some of the animals in rainforests are leopards, froogs, snakes, and spiders.  Rainforests give life to many things.

**Correctly Spelled Words:**

_____  _____

_____  _____

_____  _____

## Boost Your Learning! 🚀

Always be sure to check words that may not be spelled correctly.  To show that a word may be spelled incorrectly, draw a circle around it and write *SP*.  Then, check a dictionary or a word wall to find the correct spelling.

**Example:** Tall (tries) make up the (canipy) of the rain forest.

**NAME:** _____

**Directions:** Reread the paragraph. Then, write a concluding sentence.

A rainforest is a feast for your senses. There are beautiful plants, trees, and animals to see in rainforests. The flowers in rainforests have many smells. You can hear lots of noises made by the birds and other animals. Some plants feel smooth, while others feel quite bumpy. Some of the foods we taste, such as bananas, spices, and sugar, were first found in rainforests.

_____

_____

_____

## This week I learned:

- to match the topic and conclusion sentences
- that using synonyms makes writing more interesting
- to look out for misspelled words

NAME: _____

**Directions:** Place check marks next to the sentences that you would include in an informative/explanatory paragraph about temperate forests.

☐ 1. Many people live near temperate forests.

☐ 2. It can be lots of fun to run through forests.

☐ 3. Temperate forests have four seasons.

☐ 4. I enjoy the scenery in the forests.

☐ 5. Good soil for growing plants can be found in temperate forests.

☐ 6. Temperate forests usually get lots of rain.

☐ 7. Some people live in cabins in temperate forests.

☐ 8. It is scary to walk through temperate forests.

Drafting

Temperate Forests

**NAME:** _____

**Directions:** Describe a temperate forest. Include details about how the forest looks and smells. Use the notes from page 49 to help you.

_____

_____

_____

_____

_____

_____

_____

_____

_____

_____

## Remember!

A strong informative/ explanatory paragraph includes:

- a topic sentence
- details to support the main idea
- a concluding sentence

## Printing Practice abc

**Directions:** Use your best printing to write a title of a story that takes place in a forest.

_____

_____

NAME: _____

**Directions:** Match each word on the left with its synonym on the right. Then, create your own synonym pair.

forest

path

stream

cottage

route

cabin

woods

creek

# Time to Improve!

**Directions:** Revisit the draft you wrote on page 50. Look for repeated words, and replace them with synonyms.

Editing

Temperate Forests

NAME: _____

**Directions:** Read the paragraph. Circle the spelling errors. Then, write them on the lines below.

It can be rather spooky to visit a temperate forrest. These forests are rather dark, which makes it hard to see. Many anemals live in temperate forests, and you hear their unusual noises. The floor of a temperate forest can be damp and have a musty smel. Sometimes, shrubs or weads brush against your arms and feel strange.

_____

_____

_____

_____

## Remember!

Circle words that are spelled incorrectly and write *SP* above them. This will remind you to check with a dictionary, a word wall, or a friend to find the correct spelling.

## Time to Improve!

**Directions:** Revisit the draft you wrote on page 50 about temperate forests. Check for any misspelled words.

**NAME:** _____

**Directions:** Describe a temperate forest. Include details about how the forest looks and smells.

_____

_____

_____

_____

_____

_____

_____

_____

_____

_____

_____

**NAME:** Walter

**Directions:** Look at the jack-o-lantern. Circle whether the jack-o-lantern is scary or not scary. Then, place stars next to the sentences that support your opinion.

## My Opinion

The jack-o-lantern is:     **scary**     (**not scary**)

## Supporting Sentences

_____ The teeth are very sharp.

_✗_ It's only a pumpkin.

_____ I don't like the dark eyes.

_✗_ I wouldn't want it on my doorstep.

_✗_ The face looks like it is smiling.

NAME: _____

**Directions:** Read the paragraph.  Underline sentences that have opinions in them.

The jack-o-lantern I carved is scary.  I started with a big pumpkin, and everyone knows that big pumpkins are scarier than small pumpkins.  Then, I designed a scary face.  My jack-o-lantern has a scary mouth that looks like a frown.  There are lots of scary pointy teeth in its mouth.  Those pointy teeth look scary.  I think my jack-o-lantern is the scariest of all.

# Printing Practice abc

**Directions:** Use your best printing to write one sentence about what you like to do in the fall.

I like to JUMP in to
leaves!

**NAME:** _____

**Directions:** Read the sentences. They do not make sense. Rewrite them so that they do make sense.

1. Jack-o-lanterns are fun Valentine's Day decorations.

   Jack o lanternns are fun Halloween decorations,

2. We like to hide our jack-o-lanterns so everyone can see them.

   We like to hold our jack o lant erns so everyone can see them

3. Halloween is the best month of the year!

   Halloween is the best day month of the year!

---

**Boost Your Learning!**

It is important to reread what you have written to be sure that the words you wrote make sense. If you find something in your writing that is not clear, draw a line under it. This will remind you to go back and revise what you wrote.

**Example:** I think this confusing sentence.

---

#51525—180 Days of Writing                                        © Shell Education

**NAME:** _____

**Directions:** Read each sentence. Use the ◦ symbol to delete words that do not make sense. Write correct words above or below the words you crossed out.

1. They went to the strawberry fields to get a pumpkin to carve for Halloween.

2. Be sure your jack-o-lantern is carved and ready by September 30.

3. You might want to have an adult help cut your jack-o-lanterns because knives are usually dull.

4. People are usually very happy when they see a scary jack-o-lantern.

## Boost Your Learning!

It is important to be sure that the words you use in your writing make sense. You can show that you want to change a word that does not fit by drawing a line through it and writing a different word above or below it.

**Example:** We think that scary jack-o-lantern is cute.
frightening

**NAME:** _____

**Directions:** Read the paragraph. Then, respond to the prompt.

The jack-o-lantern I carved is scary. I started with a big pumpkin, and everyone knows that big pumpkins are scarier than small pumpkins. Then, I designed a scary face. My jack-o-lantern has a scary mouth that looks like a frown. There are lots of scary pointy teeth in its mouth. Those pointy teeth look scary. My jack-o-lantern's eyes are partly closed. That makes the face look scary. I think my jack-o-lantern is the scariest of all.

1. Write one example of a detail that supports the author's opinion.

_____

_____

## This week I learned: ✏️📝

- to find, underline and fix confusing sentences
- to identify sentences with opinion in them

**NAME:** _____

**Directions:** Look at the picture of a scarecrow. Do you think it is scary? Write your ideas in the boxes.

## Detail

## Detail

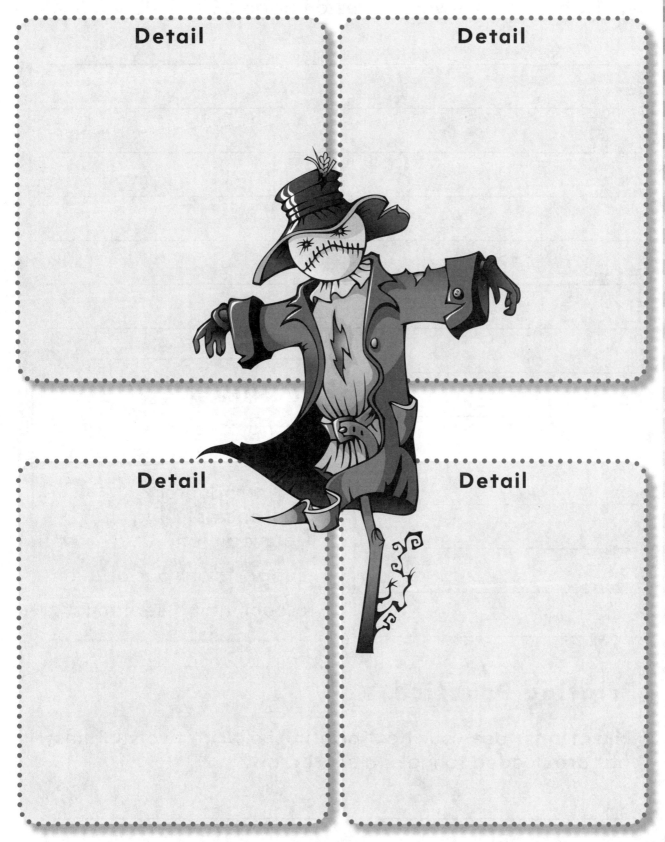

## Detail

## Detail

Drafting
Scarecrows

**NAME:** _____

**Directions:** Do you think scarecrows are scary? Draft a paragraph stating your opinion. Add details to support your opinion. Use your notes on page 59 to help you.

_____

_____

_____

_____

_____

_____

_____

_____

_____

_____

_____

_____

> ## Remember!
>
> A strong opinion paragraph includes:
>
> • an introductory sentence stating your opinion
>
> • support for your opinion
>
> • a concluding sentence

## Printing Practice abc

**Directions:** Use your best printing to write two supplies that are needed to make a scarecrow.

_____        _____

**NAME:** _____

**Directions:** Read the sentences. Decide if they make sense. Rewrite any that do not make sense.

| Sentences | Does it make sense? | New Sentences |
|---|---|---|
| **Example:** Farmers place scarecrows on their fields to welcome birds. | Y ⓝ | Farmers place scarecrows **in** their fields to **scare** the birds. |
| Scarecrows are often seen in on when the fall. | Y    N | |
| Old clothes are used to make scarecrows. | Y    N | |
| Birds usually fly up to away from scarecrows. | Y    N | |
| The arms and legs of with scarecrows wave when the wind blows. | Y    N | |

# Time to Improve!

**Directions:** Reread the draft you wrote on page 60. Rewrite sentences that do not make sense.

Editing | Scarecrows

NAME: _____

**Directions:** Read each sentence. Find the words that are used more than once. Use the _____ symbol to delete them. Then, write different words above or below them.

1. Scarecrows have scary faces and scary bodies.

2. Farmers don't want birds to eat their plants so they put scarecrows where their plants are growing.

3. Scarecrows wear old shirts, old shoes, old pants, and old hats.

4. Fall is a time when you see scarecrows, because birds like to eat the fall plants.

**Time to Improve!**

**Directions:** Reread the paragraph you wrote on page 60. Look for words that are used too often. Then, change them.

NAME: _____

**Directions:** Do you think scarecrows are scary? Write a paragraph about your opinion. Add details to help support your opinion.

_____

_____

_____

_____

_____

_____

_____

_____

_____

_____

_____

_____

Prewriting

Being Thankful

**NAME:** _____

**Directions:** Place check marks in the leaves that you would include in an opinion paragraph about being thankful.

Some people are unhappy with things they have.

People give thanks for many things.

You will feel good if you give thanks.

You should always be thankful for those around you.

You must buy lots of things to be happy.

When people do things for you, you should thank them.

Being grateful for the things you have is good.

NAME: _____

**Directions:** Read the paragraph.  Circle the opinion. Then, underline sentences that support the opinion.

People usually feel better when they are thankful. Maybe you do not like what you are having for dinner. You will feel better when you are thankful you have food.  You might think you have too much homework. If you are thankful you can learn, you will feel better. Instead of thinking your clothes are too old, be happy you have clothes, and you will feel better.  When you find a reason to be thankful, it can help you feel good.

# Printing Practice abc

**Directions:** Use your best printing to write one sentence about something that makes you thankful.

_____

_____

Revising
Being Thankful

**NAME:** _____

**Directions:** Match each phrase with its contraction. Then, write a sentence using one of the contractions.

| Phrases | Contractions |
| --- | --- |
| you are | you'll |
| you will | won't |
| you have | you're |
| will not | you've |
| where is | it's |
| it is | where's |

**Sentence with a Contraction**

_____

_____

## Boost Your Learning! 🚀

A **contraction** is a shortened version of a word or words. To make a contraction, use an apostrophe to show where letters were removed.

**Example:** *they are = they're*

**NAME:** _____

**Directions:** Use the # symbol to show where spaces need to be added between words.  Then, write a sentence telling why you are thankful.  Use correct spacing.

1. When I am thankful, I rememberthe many

   goodthings I have.

2. There are manythings that make me

   feelthankful.

3. _____

   _____

## Boost Your Learning!

Words need to have spaces between them so that the reader can see where words begin and end.  To show where to make a space, use the # symbol.

**Example:** I am thankful#for my family.

**Publishing**

Being Thankful

**NAME:** _____

**Directions:** Revisit the paragraph. Circle words that could be made into contractions and still make sense. Write them as contractions on the lines below.

> People usually feel better when they are thankful. Maybe you do not like what you are having for dinner. You will feel better when you are thankful you have food. You might think you have too much homework. If you are thankful you can learn, you will feel better. Instead of thinking your clothes are too old, be happy you have clothes and you will feel better. When you find a reason to be thankful, it can help you feel good.

_____      _____

_____      _____

_____      _____

## This week I learned: ✏️📖

- to identify the opinion and supporting details
- how to make two words into contractions
- that spaces are needed between words

**NAME:** _____

**Directions:** Write one thing you are thankful for at the top of the gift. Complete the rest of the box by telling whom you could thank and ways to share your thanks.

I am thankful for . . .

I should thank . . .

Ways to share my thanks . . .

**Drafting**

Sharing Thanks

**NAME:** _____

**Directions:** What is the best way to give thanks to someone? Explain why it is the best way. Use your notes from page 69 to help you.

_____

_____

_____

_____

_____

_____

_____

_____

_____

> **Remember!**
>
> A strong opinion paragraph includes:
>
> • an introductory sentence stating your opinion
>
> • support for your opinion
>
> • a concluding sentence

**Printing Practice** abc

**Directions:** Use your best printing to write one way you like to be thanked.

_____

_____

**NAME:** _____

**Directions:** Read the contractions. Write the two words that make each contraction in the appropriate spaces. Then, write two sentences using contractions from the list.

| Contraction | First Word | Second Word |
|-------------|------------|-------------|
| we've | we | have |
| they're | | |
| she's | | |
| wouldn't | | |
| I'll | | |
| can't | | |
| that's | | |

1. _____

_____

2. _____

_____

# Time to Improve! 

**Directions:** Go back to the draft you wrote on page 70. Look for words that could be made into contractions and change them. Remember to use apostrophes correctly.

**Editing**

Sharing Thanks

**NAME:** _____

**Directions:** Read the sentences. Find places where there is incorrect spacing. Use the # symbol to correct the spacing.

1. People canshare thanks by writing athankful note.

2. Delivering a plate of cookies isa good way to sharethanks.

3. Saying "thank you" is another wayof sharing thanks.

4. It is important toshare thanks when someone hashelped you.

5. When weshow we are thankful, we feel goodinside.

. . . . . . . . . . . . . . . . . . . . . . . . . . . . . . . . . . . . . . . . . . . .

# Time to Improve!

**Directions:** Reread your draft on page 70. Check to see if there is proper spacing between all of the words you wrote.

**NAME:** _____

**Directions:** What is the best way to give thanks to someone? Explain why it is the best way.

_____

_____

_____

_____

_____

_____

_____

_____

_____

_____

**NAME:** _____

**Directions:** Place check marks in the clouds with words that could be part of an informative/explanatory paragraph about thunderstorms.

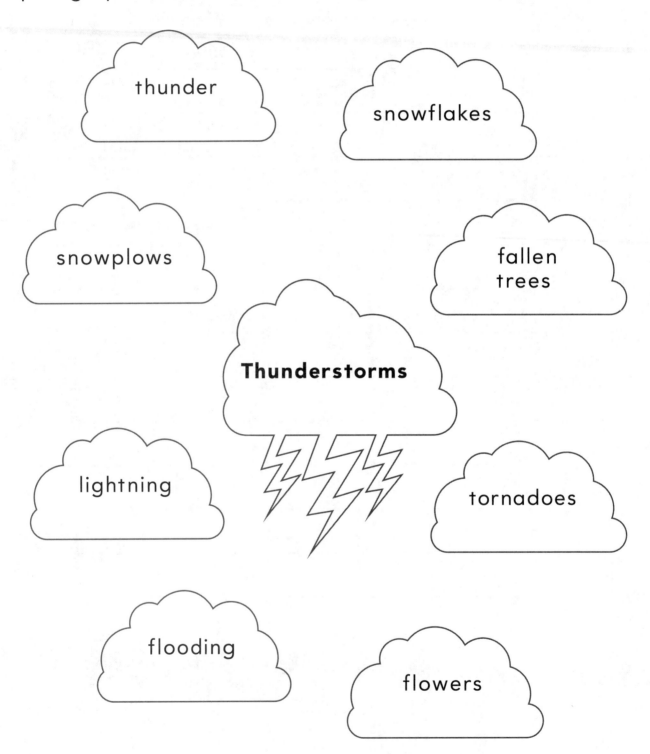

**NAME:** _____

**Directions:** Read the informative/explanatory paragraph. Circle the topic sentence. Then, underline the sentences that support the topic sentence.

Thunderstorms can be scary and dangerous. It is best to stay inside during a storm. Heavy rain during a thunderstorm can cause rivers, streams, and lakes to flood. It can be very windy during a thunderstorm. The wind might make trees fall and cause branches to blow around. Thunder is very loud. Loud noises are often frightening. Lightning can strike during a storm, and you don't want to be around that. Be sure to stay indoors during thunderstorms to be safe.

# Printing Practice abc

**Directions:** Use your best printing to write the words *thunder* and *lightning*.

_____

_____

**NAME:** _____

**Directions:** Match each topic sentence with its concluding sentence. Then, choose one pair of sentences and write a related detail sentence to support them.

| Topic Sentences | Concluding Sentences |
|---|---|
| People get very scared during thunderstorms. | If you listen carefully, the sounds will tell you what is happening. |
| Thunderstorms can be dangerous at times. | These are the reasons thunderstorms scare people. |
| Thunderstorms create loud noises. | If you are careful, you can avoid the dangers of thunderstorms. |

**My Detailed Sentence**

_____

_____

**Boost Your Learning!** 🚀

Topic and concluding sentences should say the same thing. Detail sentences should provide more information about the topic.

**NAME:** _____

**Directions:** Read the sentences. Circle the misspelled words. Then, write the words correctly on the lines.

1. Whin you see lightning, yu know you wil soon hear thunder.

_____   _____   _____

2. It can rain viry hard in the middle ov a thunderstorm.

_____   _____

3. Whne lightning flashes, it maks the sky light up.

_____   _____

4. Hail is ice thet falls form the sky during a thunderstorm.

_____   _____

## Boost Your Learning! 🚀

If you find words that have been misspelled, draw circles around them and write *SP* to remind you to fix the spelling.

**Example:** Thunderstorms mke lightning, rain, sp thunder.

Publishing
Thunderstorms

**NAME:** _____

**Directions:** Revisit the paragraph. Write your own topic and concluding sentences that match the details in the paragraph. As you write, check that the words are spelled correctly.

_____

_____

Heavy rain during a thunderstorm can cause rivers, streams, and lakes to flood. It can be very windy during a thunderstorm. The wind might make trees fall and cause branches to blow around. Thunder is very loud. Loud noises are often frightening. Lightning can strike during a storm, and you don't want to be around that.

_____

_____

_____

_____

## This week I learned: 🖊️

- that topic and concluding sentences should be similar

- that detail sentences should support the topic and concluding sentences

- to check that words are spelled correctly

**NAME:** _____

**Directions:** Place check marks in the snowflakes that tell about snowstorms.

**Drafting**

Snowstorms

**NAME:** _____

**Directions:** Describe what a snowstorm is. Include details about what it looks like and the dangers it can cause. Use the notes from page 79 to help you.

_____

_____

_____

_____

_____

_____

_____

_____

_____

_____

**Remember!**

- Your topic and concluding sentences should be similar.

- Write detail sentences that support the topic.

# Printing Practice abc

**Directions:** Use your best printing to write two things you can do in the snow.

_____

_____

**NAME:** _____

**Directions:** Write a topic or concluding sentence to match the sentences already written.

**Topic Sentence:** There are many things you can do outdoors after a snowstorm.

**Concluding Sentence:** _____

_____

_____

---

**Topic Sentence:** _____

_____

_____

**Concluding Sentence:** So remember to be careful when you are outside during a snowstorm.

## Time to Improve!

**Directions:** Revisit the draft you wrote on page 80. Do your topic and concluding sentences match? If they do not, rewrite them.

Editing
Snowstorms

**NAME:** _____

**Directions:** Each sentence is missing a word. Use the ∧ symbol to add the best word from the Word Bank to each sentence.

### Word Bank

| | | |
|---|---|---|
| were | often | from |
| quiet | another | there |

1. We going to have hot cocoa after sledding.

2. The snow is so when it falls, it does not make a sound.

3. Look over and see the snowman they made.

4. She got a new hat her grandmother.

5. Our school closes because of bad weather.

6. Would anyone like cookie?

## Time to Improve!

**Directions:** Look at the draft you wrote on page 80. Circle any words that are misspelled or do not make sense and correct them.

**NAME:** _____

**Directions:** Describe what a snowstorm is. Include details about what it looks like and the dangers it can cause.

_____

_____

_____

_____

_____

_____

_____

_____

_____

_____

**NAME:** _____

**Directions:** Place check marks in the gifts that you would like to receive.

#51525—180 Days of Writing © Shell Education

**NAME:** _____

**Directions:** Read the narrative paragraph. Circle the words that express feelings.

> Of all the gifts I received at my party, I will always remember the one from my little sister. Early in the month, my sister bought me a book that she knew I would like. She knew I'd like it because I have other books by the same author. My mom said my sister was so happy when she brought the book home and wrapped it. On the day of the party, my sister was anxious to give me my gift. As I opened the gift, my sister was smiling, laughing, and jumping up and down. I loved the gift, and I loved seeing my sister so happy, excited, and joyful.

# Printing Practice abc

**Directions:** Use your best printing to write one sentence about a great present you have received.

_____

_____

Revising

Gifts to Me

**NAME:** _____

**Directions:** Look at the two situations. List three words that tell how you might feel in each one.

It was a Saturday. There was new snow outside, and my parents gave me a new sled.

_____

_____

_____

The puzzle I got was missing six pieces, so we had to get a new one.

_____

_____

_____

## Boost Your Learning! 🚀

Words that show feelings and emotions make your writing more interesting. Use these words to add excitement to your writing.

**NAME:** _____

**Directions:** Use the ∧ symbol to add commas to the sentences.

1. I usually get presents on my birthday at Christmas and for Valentine's Day.

2. We get hats scarves and mittens for winter.

3. My brother had a hockey stick ice skates and a sled on his gift list.

4. My dog got bones squeaky toys and treats on his birthday.

5. Our teacher receives notes pictures and hugs at school.

## Boost Your Learning!

Use commas to separate three or more ideas in a sentence.

**Example:** The best gifts I've received were a new book an art set and a gift card for the toy store.

**NAME:** _____

**Directions:** Read the narrative paragraph. Then, answer the question below.

Of all the gifts I received at Christmas, I will always remember the one from my little sister. Early in December my sister bought me a book that she knew I would like. She knew I'd like it because I have other books by the same author. My mom said my sister was so happy when she brought the book home, wrapped it, and put it under the tree. On Christmas, my sister was anxious to give me my gift. As I opened the gift, my sister was smiling, laughing, and jumping up and down. I loved the gift, and I loved seeing my sister so happy, excited, and joyful.

1. Does the author do a good job at using feeling words? Explain.

_____

_____

**This week I learned:** ✏️📒

- to add commas to a series of three or more items
- to add words that express feelings

**NAME:** _____

**Directions:** Write the names of two people to whom you have given gifts. Then, write words that tell how you felt when you gave the gifts.

**To:** _____

**I gave:** _____

**How I felt when I gave this gift:**

_____

**To:** _____

**I gave:** _____

**How I felt when I gave this gift:**

_____

Drafting

Giving to Others

**NAME:** _____

**Directions:** Think about a time you gave someone a gift. Draft a narrative about what the gift was, how you picked it out, and how the person reacted when they opened it. Use your notes on page 89 to help you.

_____

_____

_____

_____

_____

_____

_____

_____

_____

> ## Remember! 
> A strong narrative paragraph includes a beginning, a middle, and an end.

## Printing Practice abc

**Directions:** Use your best printing to write why you like giving gifts.

_____

_____

**NAME:** _____

Revising
Giving to Others

**Directions:** It is important to use different feeling words in a narrative. Write the words from the Feeling Word Bank in the appropriate boxes below.

**Feeling Word Bank**

| eager | joyful | grateful | satisfied |
| anxious | pleased | glad | enthusiastic |
| cheerful | contented | thrilled | energized |

**Happy**

**Excited**

**Thankful**

# Time to Improve! 

**Directions:** Reread your draft on page 90. Add different feeling words to help readers understand your emotions.

Editing

Giving to Others

NAME: _____

**Directions:** Read the sentences. Use the ∧ symbol to add commas to the sentences.

1. My friend got games puzzles and books for her birthday.

2. We need to prepare invitations snacks and games for the party.

3. My grandma says the best gifts are hugs smiles and cuddles.

4. I can't wait to give gifts to my friend my dad and my sister.

## Remember!

Add commas to a series of three or more objects.

## Time to Improve!

**Directions:** Go back to the draft you wrote on page 90. Look for places that might be missing commas. Add commas where necessary.

**NAME:** _____

**Directions:** Think about a time you gave someone a gift. Write a narrative about what the gift was, how you picked it out, and how the person reacted when they opened it.

_____

_____

_____

_____

_____

_____

_____

_____

_____

_____

_____

**NAME:** _____

**Directions:** Each of the pictures below can be used to build a snowman. Label each picture.

1. _____

2. _____

3. _____

4. _____

5. _____

6. _____

NAME: _____

**Directions:** The narrative below is out of order. Write numbers in front of the sentences to show the correct order. **Note:** The first and last sentences are correct.

The snow had just stopped, and my friend came over to play. _____It was a great day to build a snowman. _____We got a carrot and some large buttons from my mom and used them to make a nose, eyes, and mouth. _____We rolled a small snowball for the snowman's head. _____We rolled a big snowball and set it in the middle of our yard. _____We got sticks for arms and an old hat and scarf. _____We rolled a medium-size snowball and set it on top of the large snowball. _____We bundled up and hurried outside to get started. Then, we went inside and drank hot cocoa as we proudly watched our snowman.

## Printing Practice abc

**Directions:** Use your best printing to write the words *snowman* and *cold*.

_____

_____

**Revising**

Building Snowmen

**NAME:** _____

**Directions:** Look at each picture. Write two different verbs to tell what is happening in each one. Choose one picture and write a sentence about what is happening below. Circle the verb in your sentence.

_____

_____

_____

_____

**My Winter Activity Sentence**

_____

_____

## Boost Your Learning!

Use a variety of action verbs in your writing to help tell what is happening.

**NAME:** _____

**Directions:** Read the paragraph. The sequence words are not spelled correctly. Use the ⟋ symbol to delete them. Then, write the correct spellings above the words.

We spent a lot of time playing outside. When we came in, we were hungry and wanted a snack. Fist, we took off our snow clothes and hung them up to dry. Secend, we looked in the cupboard for a snack. Thurd, we decided to make hot cocoa. Forth, we poured milk into a mug. The fifh thing we did was heat the milk. Our sisth job was to stir the cocoa powder into the warm milk. Marshmallows were added sevanth. Eight, we enjoyed a yummy cup of cocoa.

## Boost Your Learning! 🚀

Correctly spelled sequence words help the reader know when events happen in a story.

Publishing

Building Snowmen

**NAME:** _____

**Directions:** Revisit the narrative paragraph. Then, answer the question.

The snow had just stopped, and my friend came over to play. It was a great day to build a snowman. We bundled up and hurried outside to get started. We rolled a big snowball and set it in the middle of our yard. We rolled a medium-size snowball and set it on top of the large snowball. We rolled a small snowball for the snowman's head. We got a carrot and some large buttons from my mom and used them to make a nose, eyes, and mouth. We got sticks for arms and an old hat and scarf. Then, we went inside and drank hot cocoa as we proudly watched our snowman.

1. What makes this paragraph a strong narrative?

_____

_____

_____

**This week I learned:**

- that sequence words need to be spelled correctly
- to use interesting action verbs to help tell a story

**NAME:** _____

**Directions:** Brainstorm ideas for a narrative about sledding.

**Sledding**

**Clothes to Wear Sledding**

**Best Places to Sled**

**What I Do When I'm Sledding**

Drafting    Sledding

NAME: _____

**Directions:** Describe a time you have either gone sledding or what you think sledding might be like. Include details about the day.  Use your notes from page 99 to help you.

_____

_____

_____

_____

_____

_____

_____

_____

_____

_____

> ## Remember! 🖐
>
> A strong narrative paragraph tells a story with a beginning, a middle, and an end.

## Printing Practice abc

**Directions:** Use your best printing to describe what sledding might feel like.

_____

_____

NAME: _____

**Directions:** Write action verbs around the image to tell what is happening.  Then, write a sentence about sledding using at least two of your action verbs.

**My Sentence About Sledding**

_____

_____

_____

# Time to Improve! 

**Directions:** Reread the draft you wrote on page 100. Look for places to add interesting action verbs.  Write them in your story.

Editing · Sledding

NAME: _____

**Directions:** Read the sentences. The sequence words are not spelled correctly. Use the ⟋ symbol to delete them. Write the correct words above them.

1. Fist, I brushed my teeth.

2. Thin, my sister made us breakfast.

3. Aftor, we put on warm clothes.

4. Nexxt, we went to the park.

5. Finallee, we had fun sledding.

**Remember!**

It is important to correctly spell sequence words.

**Time to Improve!**

**Directions:** Look back at the paragraph you wrote on page 100. Check to see if you used sequence words. If they are not spelled correctly, correct them.

NAME: _____

**Directions:** Describe a time you have either gone sledding or what you think sledding might be like. Include details about the day.

_____

_____

_____

_____

_____

_____

_____

_____

_____

_____

_____

_____

**NAME:** _____

**Directions:** Place check marks in the circles that could be part of an informational/explanatory paragraph about zebras.

Zebras live in Africa.

Each zebra has a different stripe pattern.

Young zebras are foals.

Baby elephants are called calves.

Zebras are closely related to horses and donkeys.

Zebras are herbivores; they eat plants.

A group of zebras is called a herd.

A baseball team has tigers as their mascot.

**NAME:** _____

**Directions:** Read the paragraph. Underline the topic and concluding sentences. Cross out any sentences that do not support the topic of zebras.

There are so many things to learn about zebras. Zebras live in Africa. It is very hot and dry in Africa. They like to stay in family groups that are called herds. The herds travel together to find grass to eat and water to drink. Baby goats can stand just hours after they are born. Zebras use their teeth to bite and chew grass. Giraffes have very long necks. A zebra's teeth keep growing all through its life. Each zebra's stripes are in a unique pattern. No two zebras have the same pattern of stripes. Did you know all these facts about zebras?

# Printing Practice abc

**Directions:** Use your best printing to write a sentence about zebras.

_____

_____

Revising | Zebras

**NAME:** _____

**Directions:** Read the original sentence. Write a list of adjectives about zebras. Use your adjectives to rewrite the sentence.

**Original Sentence**

Zebras have stripes.

## Adjectives about Zebras

_____     _____

_____     _____

_____     _____

_____     _____

## My New and Improved Sentence

_____

_____

_____

**Remember!**

Add adjectives to nouns to liven up your writing.

**NAME:** _____

**Directions:** Read each list of words to find words that do not belong. Use the ⟋ symbol to show which words should be deleted.

1. oceans, rivers, lakes, houses, streams, airports

2. deserts, crayons, forests, lions, mountains, jungles

3. city, horse, village, town, community, book

4. brother, pizza, niece, bus, aunt, grandmother

5. bananas, apples, oranges, computers, grapes, pencils

## Boost Your Learning! 🚀

When you are writing, your ideas should be about the same topic. Delete words or sentences that are off topic.

**Example:** My mom saw elephants, zebras, a new purse, and giraffes on a safari in Africa.

Publishing | Zebras

**NAME:** _____

**Directions:** Revisit the paragraph. Then, answer the question.

There are so many things to learn about zebras. Zebras live in Africa. It is very hot and dry in Africa. They like to stay in family groups that are called herds. The herds travel together to find grass to eat and water to drink. Baby goats can stand hours after they are born. Zebras have sharp teeth for biting and chewing grass. Giraffes have very long necks. A zebra's teeth keep growing all through its life. Each zebra's stripes are a unique pattern. No two zebras have the same pattern of stripes. Did you know all these facts about zebras?

1. Does the paragraph stay on topic? How do you know?

_____

_____

## This week I learned: 🖊📏

- the detail sentences should support the topic
- to write more lively with adjectives
- how to remove words and sentences that are off topic

**NAME:** _____

**Directions:** Place check marks in the icebergs with facts about penguins.

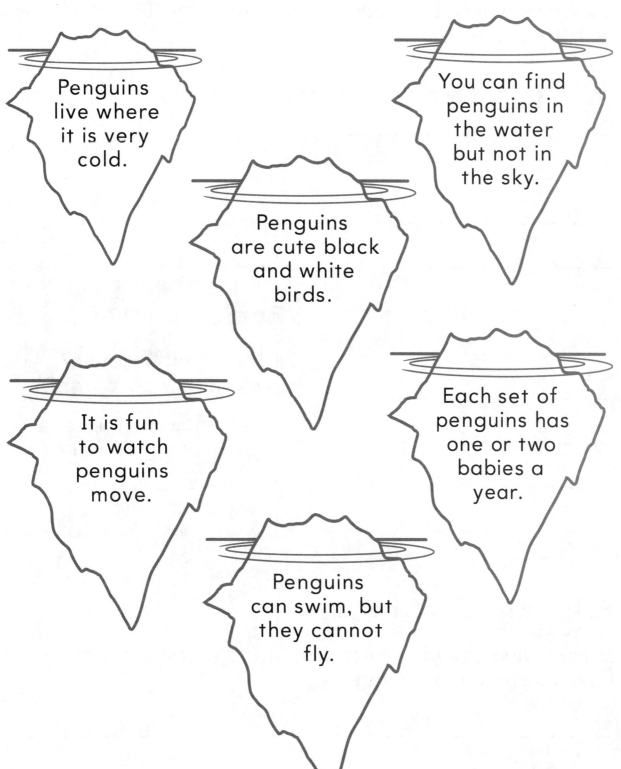

Penguins live where it is very cold.

You can find penguins in the water but not in the sky.

Penguins are cute black and white birds.

It is fun to watch penguins move.

Each set of penguins has one or two babies a year.

Penguins can swim, but they cannot fly.

**Drafting** Penguins

NAME: _____

**Directions:** Draft a paragraph about penguins. Include facts about where they live and their physical characteristics. Use your notes from page 109 to help you.

_____

_____

_____

_____

_____

_____

_____

_____

**Remember!**

A strong informative/ explanatory paragraph:

• has introductory and concluding sentences

• uses details to support the main idea

## Printing Practice abc

**Directions:** Use your best printing to write one fact you have learned about penguins.

_____

_____

**NAME:** _____

**Directions:** Look at the picture. List six adjectives that describe penguins. Then, write one sentence about penguins using adjectives from your list.

**My List of Adjectives**

_____  _____

_____  _____

_____  _____

**My Penguin Sentence**

1. _____

_____

## Time to Improve!

**Directions:** Reread the draft you wrote on page 110. Find places where you can add adjectives to make your writing more exciting.

Editing · Penguins

NAME: _____

**Directions:** Read the sentences. Find places where words are not in the correct order. Use the ⌣ symbol to show the correct order. The first one is done for you.

1. Penguins can be playful quite.

2. Penguins spend time the in water and on land.

3. Father penguins care eggs for during the winter.

4. Baby penguins stay their with parents for about six months.

# Time to Improve!

**Directions:** Reread the draft you wrote on page 110. Check that all the words in each sentence are in the correct order. Use the ⌣ symbol to show where you want to change word order.

**NAME:** _____

**Directions:** Write a paragraph about penguins. Include facts about where they live and their physical characteristics.

_____

_____

_____

_____

_____

_____

_____

_____

_____

_____

_____

_____

_____

**NAME:** _____

**Directions:** Match each important person to the detail that made them famous.

| Important People | Detail |
| --- | --- |
| | |

Thomas Edison

Amelia Earhart

Abraham Lincoln

Ruby Bridges

16th president of the United States; he helped get rid of slavery

inventor of the motion-picture camera and electric lightbulb

first African American child in Louisiana to attend an all-white school

first female pilot to fly alone across the Atlantic Ocean

**NAME:** _____

**Directions:** Read the paragraph. Circle the opinion statement. Underline the names of the important people.

Everyone should learn more about these great Americans. These are some of the greatest. Thomas Edison was an inventor. He invented many things. Amelia Earhart was a pilot who loved to fly. Abraham Lincoln fought to make life better for all American people. Ruby Bridges was brave when she helped change schools. These important people and the things they did are worth knowing about.

# Printing Practice abc

**Directions:** Use your best printing to write a sentence about one person from above.

_____

_____

**Revising**

Important People

**NAME:** _____

**Directions:** Read the statements. Write an *F* by the facts and an *O* by the opinions. Then, write your opinion statements about two important people below.

_____ Helen Keller learned to communicate even though she was blind and deaf.

_____ I think Martin Luther King Jr. was a great American.

_____ The best thing about George Washington is that he was the first president.

_____ Martin Luther King Jr. helped change the way people were treated.

_____ Sally Ride was the first American woman to travel in space.

**My Opinions**

1. _____

_____

_____

2. _____

_____

_____

**NAME:** _____

**Directions:** Use the ∧ symbol to add words to the sentences to make them opinions.

1. Dr. Seuss is an American author who wrote over 60 books.

2. Shaquille O'Neil is well known for playing basketball.

3. The airplane was invented by Americans Orville and Wilber Wright.

Wilbur          Orville

The Wright Brothers

## Boost Your Learning! 🚀

When writing an opinion sentence, you need to use words that express your opinion.

**Example:** Alexander Graham Bell is known as the inventor of the telephone.
                                        ∧
                              , the greatest American,

NAME: _____

**Directions:** Revisit the paragraph.  Add sentences that provide more information about the important people.

Everyone should learn more about these great Americans.  Thomas Edison was an inventor. _____

_____

_____

Amelia Earhart was a pilot who loved to fly. _____

_____

_____

Abraham Lincoln fought to make life better for all Americans. _____

_____

Ruby Bridges was brave when she helped change schools. _____

_____

These important people are worth knowing about.

## This week I learned:

- to identify opinions and facts
- how to insert more information in my writing

**NAME:** _____

**Directions:** Read the facts about the two places. Form an opinion about which place you would like to visit. Write your opinion below.

---

**Mount Rushmore Facts**

- located in South Dakota

- faces of four U.S. presidents carved in stone

- there are many opportunities for hiking and exploring in the surrounding area

- the carving was completed in 1941

---

**U.S.S. *Constitution* Facts**

- located in Boston, MA

- oldest U.S. naval ship still floating

- first sailed in 1797

- many other historical sites to see within walking distance of the U.S.S. *Constitution*

---

**My opinion of where I would like to visit . . .**

_____

_____

_____

**Drafting**

Important Places

**NAME:** _____

**Directions:** Write a paragraph about a place that is important to you. Include details such as where it is located. Use the ideas on page 119 to help you.

_____

_____

_____

_____

_____

_____

_____

_____

_____

_____

## Remember! 

A strong opinion paragraph:

* has an introductory and a concluding sentence stating your opinion

* gives reasons that support the opinion

* uses capital letters when naming specific places

## Printing Practice abc

**Directions:** Use your best printing to write the names of two important places.

_____

_____

**NAME:** _____

**Directions:** Read the sentences. Circle the words that let you know that each statement is an opinion.

1. I prefer going to the zoo in our city.

2. I think the best place to visit is Boston, MA.

3 The best thing about my town is the carnival we have every year.

4. Everyone should take a vacation to California.

5. It is better to go to Washington, D.C., than Florida.

**Time to Improve!** 🏅

**Directions:** Reread the draft you wrote on page 120. Find places where you need to add opinion statements. Use the ∧ symbol to show where you want your new opinion statements to go.

Editing

Important Places

**NAME:** _____

**Directions:** Use the ≡ symbol to show where capital letters are needed in the following sentences.

1. Our favorite building in washington, D.C., is the washington memorial.

2. We thought the old north church was the most interesting place to see in boston.

3. The giant sequoia trees in yosemite national park are fun to see.

4. My family thinks our trip to the grand canyon was our best one ever.

5. Everyone should go to the alamo in texas.

6. My favorite vacation was to mount rushmore.

**Remember!**

Names of specific places need to be capitalized.

**Time to Improve!**

**Directions:** Reread your draft on page 120. Check to see if you capitalized the names of specific places.

**NAME:** _____

**Directions:** Write a paragraph about a place that is important to you. Include details such as where it is located.

_____

_____

_____

_____

_____

_____

_____

_____

_____

_____

_____

_____

**NAME:** _____

**Directions:** Circle the elements that are part of the story *Little Red Riding Hood*.

### Setting

forest    city    town    woods    desert    beach

### Characters

bear        grandmother        mother        witch
hunter      little girl        wolf          fairy

### Props

red hood    basket    food    stones    flowers

**NAME:** _____

**Directions:** Read this version of *Little Red Riding Hood*. Underline places where people in the story are speaking.

There is a girl called Little Red Hoodie because she wears red hoodies every day. One afternoon, her mother says, "Please take this dinner to your grandmother." As she rides her bike towards her grandmother's house, she meets a woman.

"What is in your basket?" the woman asks.

Little Red Hoodie says, "It's dinner for my grandmother." The lady asks where her grandmother lives, Little Red Hoodie tells her, and they go on their way.

Little Red Hoodie arrives at the house and sees the woman she met on the way. Little Red Hoodie says, "Where is my grandma?"

The woman tells her, "Your grandma left and told me to eat her dinner." Little Red Hoodie hears a noise from the other room, opens the door, and sees her grandmother resting in bed. Little Red Hoodie was very confused.

# Printing Practice ᵃᵇᶜ

**Directions:** Write the words: *Little Red Hoodie.*

_____

**Revising**

Little Red Riding Hood

**NAME:** _____

**Directions:** Read the classic endings to these stories. Write a different ending for each.

## The Three Little Pigs

**Classic Story Ending:** The wolf cannot blow down the house made of brick, and the three pigs are safe.

**Modern Story Ending:** _____

_____

_____

## Little Red Hen

**Classic Story Ending:** All the animals who refused to help before want to help Little Red Hen eat the bread, but she says, "No, no!  I will do that."

**Modern Story Ending:** _____

_____

_____

### Boost Your Learning!

Stories' endings should contain the solutions to the problems and let the reader know what happens to the characters.

**NAME:** _____

**Directions:** Use the ∨ symbol to add quotation marks to the sentences.

1. The old woman said, I am going to catch that runaway cookie!

2. We are looking for someone to help us make bread, said the animals.

. . . . . . . . . . . . . . . . . . . . . . . . . . . . . . . . . . . . . . . . .

**Directions:** Circle the sentences that have used quotation marks correctly.

Goldilocks says, "This chair is too soft."

The wolf knocked on the door of the house and said

to the little pigs, Let me in!

The prince asked, "Who is the owner of this

glass slipper?"

## Boost Your Learning!

Use quotation marks to show when someone is speaking.

**Example:** 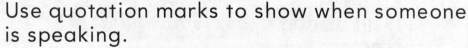 The hare told the tortoise, I will win the race!

Publishing

Little Red Riding Hood

**NAME:** _____

**Directions:** Reread the last part of *Little Red Riding Hood*. Write your own conclusion for this version of the story.

Little Red Hoodie arrives at the house and sees the woman she met on the way. Little Red Hoodie said, "Where is my grandma?"

The woman tells her, "Your grandma left and told me to eat her dinner." Little Red Hoodie hears a noise from the other room, opens the door and sees her grandmother resting in bed. Little Red Hoodie was very confused.

_____

_____

_____

_____

_____

**This week I learned:**

- that quotation marks show what characters say
- a story needs an ending that tells how the problems of the story are solved

**NAME:** _____

**Directions:** Brainstorm the characters, setting, and events for your own version of *Goldilocks and the Three Bears*.

| Goldilocks and the Three Bears | |
| --- | --- |
| **Classic Story** | **Modern Story** |
| **Characters**<br><br>Goldilocks    Mama Bear<br><br>Papa Bear    Baby Bear | **Characters** |
| **Setting**<br><br>Cottage    Summer<br><br>Woods | **Setting** |
| **Plot**<br><br>The bears' porridge is too hot, so they go for a walk.<br><br>Goldilocks visits their house and eats the porridge, breaks a chair, and falls asleep.<br><br>The bears come home and find their house a mess and Goldilocks sleeping.<br><br>Goldilocks runs away from the bears' house. | **Plot** |

Drafting

Goldilocks and the Three Bears

**NAME:** _____

**Directions:** Draft a modern version of *Goldilocks and the Three Bears*. Include dialogue and a strong conclusion. Use your notes from page 129 to help you.

_____

_____

_____

_____

_____

_____

_____

_____

_____

_____

> ## Remember! ✎
>
> A strong narrative paragraph:
>
> - includes an introductory and a concluding sentence
>
> - uses sensory details to describe the experience
>
> - makes it sound like a story

## Printing Practice abc

**Directions:** Use your best printing to write the names of two characters from your story.

_____

_____

NAME: _____

**Directions:** Tell what each character in your story is doing at the end. Use the information to write a strong concluding sentence for your story.

| My Modern *Goldilocks and the Three Bears* ||
|---|---|
| **Characters** | **What they are doing at the end of the story?** |
| | |
| | |
| | |
| | |

**My concluding sentence:**

_____

_____

_____

## Time to Improve! ⚜

**Directions:** Reread the draft you wrote on page 130. Does your ending tell what all the characters are doing? Add more information to your conclusion, if needed.

Editing
Goldilocks and the Three Bears

**NAME:** _____

**Directions:** Use the ∨ symbol to add quotation marks to the answers.

---

**Question:** What is your favorite fairy tale?

**Answer:** Jordan told me, My favorite fairy tale is *The Gingerbread Man.*

---

**Question:** Why do you think Goldilocks goes into the bears' house?

**Answer:** I think Goldilocks is cold, so she goes into the bears' house to get warm, answered Emily.

---

**Question:** What do you think the bears should do when they find Goldilocks sleeping?

**Answer:** Cally said, I think the bears should let Goldilocks finish her nap and give her a snack.

---

## Time to Improve!

**Directions:** Look back at the draft you wrote on page 130. Check to see if you used quotation marks correctly.

**NAME:** _____

**Directions:** Write a modern version of *Goldilocks and the Three Bears*. Include dialogue and a strong conclusion.

_____

_____

_____

_____

_____

_____

_____

_____

_____

_____

_____

_____

_____

**NAME:** _____

**Directions:** Place check marks in the lily pads with facts about what frogs look like.

Frogs are slimy.

Tree frogs have pads on their feet.

Some frogs have spotted skin.

**Frogs**

Everyone thinks frogs are cute.

Frogs that live in water have webbed feet.

Frogs have large eyes.

Toads are sometimes mistaken for frogs.

Frogs are shades of green.

**NAME:** _____

Drafting

Frogs

**Directions:** Read the paragraph.  Underline sentences that describe what frogs look like.

Not all frogs look the same.  Frogs can be many different colors.  Some frogs are green or brown to blend in with their surroundings.  Frogs begin their lives as tadpoles.  Poison dart frogs are colorful to let predators know to stay away.  Frogs range in size from less than one inch (2.54 centimeters) to more than 12 inches (30 centimeters) long.  There are many endangered frogs in the world.  Most frogs have big eyes that let them see all around.  Some people think that a frog will turn into a prince when it is kissed.  Frogs have different types of feet.  Webbed feet help frogs living in water swim.  Pads on their fingers and toes help tree frogs climb.  The different appearances make frogs interesting to see.

## Printing Practice abc

**Directions:** Use your best printing to write the words *bullfrog*, *tree frog*, *goliath frog*, and *poison dart frog*.

_____

_____

_____

Revising | Frogs

**NAME:** _____

**Directions:** Add adjectives to each noun. Then, select one noun and write a descriptive sentence about frogs.

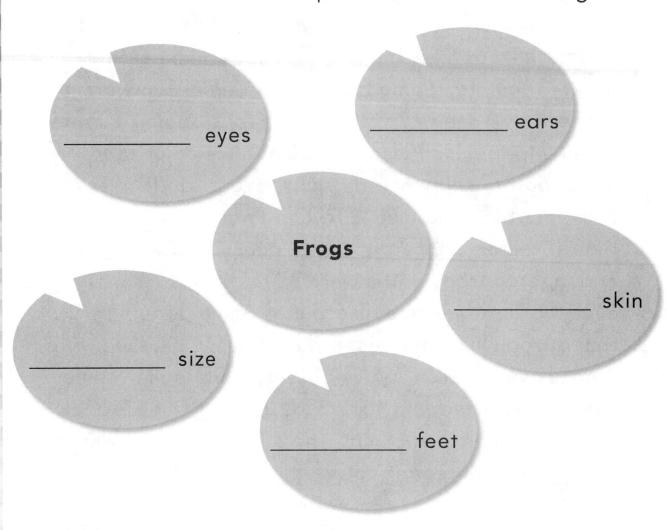

_____ eyes

_____ ears

**Frogs**

_____ skin

_____ size

_____ feet

## My Descriptive Frog Sentence

_____

_____

## Remember!

Use adjectives when you write to create vivid pictures for the reader.

NAME: _____

**Directions:** Read each sentence. Use the lowercase symbol / to show which capital letters need to be lowercase.

1. Strong back Legs and Webbed feet Help frogs swim.

2. Humans are Helped by frogs because Frogs eat Insects.

3. Each species of frog Makes its own Special sound.

4. Tadpoles go Through several Stages before they are Adult frogs.

5. Pads on their fingers and toes help Tree Frogs climb.

## Boost Your Learning! 🚀

Keep in mind that the first word in a sentence and proper nouns (nouns that name people, places, or things) should be capitalized.

**Example:** A Baby frog is Called a tadpole.

NAME: _____

**Directions:** Read the informative/explanatory paragraph. Then, answer the question below.

Not all frogs look the same. Frogs can be many different colors. Some frogs are green or brown to blend in with their surroundings. Frogs begin their lives as tadpoles. Poison dart frogs are colorful to let predators know to stay away. Frogs range in size from less than one inch (2.54 centimeters) to more than 12 inches (30 centimeters) long. There are many endangered frogs in the world. Most frogs have big eyes that let them see all around. Some people think that a frog will turn into a prince when it is kissed. Frogs have different types of feet. Webbed feet help frogs living in water swim. Pads on their fingers and toes help tree frogs climb. The different appearances make frogs interesting to see.

**1.** Does the paragraph stay on topic? Explain.

_____

_____

## This week I learned: 🖊✏️

- detail sentences need to relate to the topic
- using adjectives can make writing more vivid
- capital letters should be used for the beginnings of sentences and proper nouns

NAME: _____

**Directions:** Circle the turtles with information that could be included in an informative/explanatory paragraph about turtles.

Turtles lay eggs.

Turtles are reptiles.

Turtles are rather strange looking.

Turtles are cold blooded.

Turtles have upper and lower shells.

Turtle shells have different designs.

Some turtles live on land and others in water.

My brother likes turtles.

Drafting  Turtles

**NAME:** _____

**Directions:** Explain what turtles look like. Provide descriptive details using various adjectives. Use the notes from page 139 to help you.

_____

_____

_____

_____

_____

_____

_____

_____

_____

_____

_____

## Remember!

A strong informative/ explanatory paragraph should:

- include only relevant information

- have an introductory and a concluding sentence

- use details to support the topic

## Printing Practice abc

**Directions:** Use your best printing to write the name of a place where you have seen a turtle.

_____

**NAME:** _____

**Directions:** Look at the turtle. Brainstorm adjectives to describe it. Then, write one sentence about the turtle using adjectives from your list.

**My List of Adjectives**

_____     _____

_____     _____

_____     _____

**My Turtle Sentence**

_____

_____

_____

## Time to Improve! ✎

**Directions:** Review the draft you wrote on page 140. Did you use different adjectives? Add new ones from the list above to liven up your writing.

Editing · Turtles

NAME: _____

**Directions:** Read the sentences. Find words that are not capitalized correctly. Use the / symbol to show they should be lowercase.

1. The Sea Turtles live in the Pacific Ocean.

2. The children searched for turtles at the Beach.

3. My Sister is doing a research report on turtles for her class at School.

4. On Tuesday, we are going on a Field Trip to an Aquarium.

. . . . . . . . . . . . . . . . . . . . . . . . . . . . . . . . . . . . . . . . . . . . . . .

# Time to Improve!

**Directions:** Reread your draft on page 140. Check to be sure you used correct capitalization. If you see any errors, correct them.

NAME: _____

**Directions:** Explain what turtles look like. Provide descriptive details using various adjectives.

_____

_____

_____

_____

_____

_____

_____

_____

_____

_____

_____

_____

_____

_____

NAME: _____

**Directions:** Place check marks in the planets with characters and places that you might find in a story about planets.

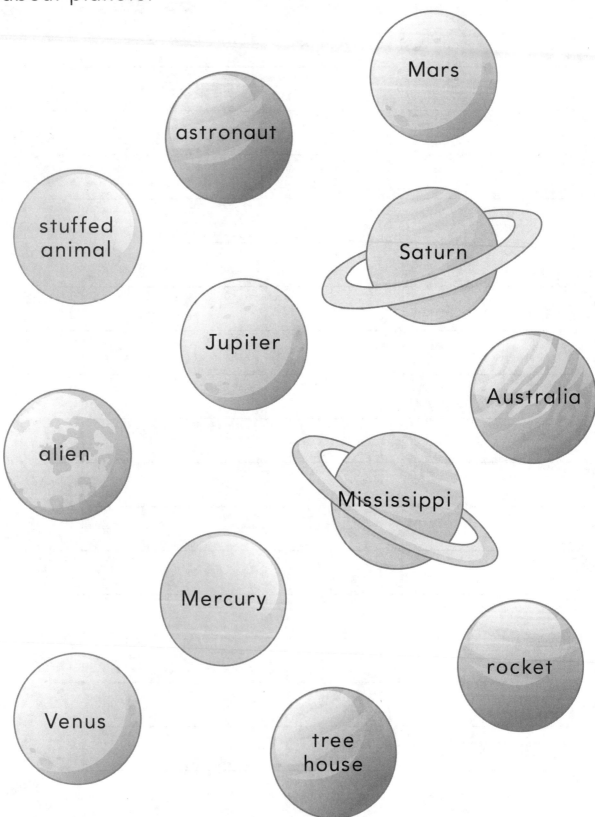

NAME: _____

**Directions:** Read the story.  Circle the characters.
Underline the names of places the characters go.

An astronaut decided to take a trip to the planets.
He blasted off from Earth in his rocket and shot up
into the sky.  The astronaut stopped at Mercury and
found it was close to the sun and was too hot.  So he
went on.  On Venus, he met a nice alien.  They became
friends and decided to travel together.  The astronaut
and alien skipped over Earth and visited Mars and
then Jupiter.  They spent a long time exploring the
big red spot on Jupiter and tried to walk around
it.  The rings of Saturn confused the friends, so they
went on to see Uranus and
Neptune.  After Neptune,
they were both tired, so
the astronaut took the
alien back to Venus before
heading home to Earth.

# Printing Practice abc

**Directions:** Use your best printing to write the names of
two planets from above.

_____    _____

Revising   Planets

NAME: _____

**Directions:** Read the sentences. Rewrite each sentence and add details to make it more interesting.

**Sentence:** The astronaut traveled in space.

**Detailed Sentence:** _____

_____

_____

**Sentence:** He found an alien on the planet.

**Detailed Sentence:** _____

_____

_____

## Boost Your Learning!

When you **elaborate**, you give more information about the characters, setting, or activities in your story. Providing extra details to your writing makes it more exciting to read!

**NAME:** _____

**Directions:** List four sequence words. Then, use the ∧ symbol to add sequence words to the paragraph below.

---

### My Sequence Words

_____  _____

_____  _____

---

The astronaut and alien were excited to explore Jupiter. They looked for the red spot. They walked all around the red spot and tried to figure out what made it. The astronaut and alien searched for a lake. They climbed in and out of craters. They got tired and decided to take a rest back on their spaceship.

---

## Boost Your Learning! 🚀

Sequence words help the reader to understand the order of your story.

**Example:** First, ∧The astronaut and alien looked at each other and decided to explore. ∧then

**NAME:** _____

**Directions:** Revisit the text. Use the ∧ symbol to add words that elaborate on the characters, setting, and plot.

An astronaut decided to take a trip to visit the planets. He blasted off from Earth in his rocket and shot up into the sky. The astronaut stopped at Mercury and found it was close to the sun and was too hot, so he went on. On Venus, he met a nice alien. They became friends and decided to travel together. The astronaut and alien skipped over Earth and visited Mars and then Jupiter. They spent a long time exploring the big red spot on Jupiter and tried to walk around it. The rings of Saturn confused the friends, so they went on to see Uranus and Neptune. After Neptune, they were both ready to go home, so the astronaut took the alien back to Venus before heading home to Earth.

## This week I learned:

- to elaborate on the characters, setting, and plot
- to use sequence words to help tell a story

**NAME:** _____

**Directions:** Complete the sentence. Then, fill in the chart with information for a narrative about where you would like to visit.

I would like to visit _____ .

(the sun     the moon     the stars)

| I am going to visit _____. | | |
| --- | --- | --- |
| **What it will look like:** | **How I will feel:** | **What I will do there:** |
| | | |

**Drafting**

Sun, Moon, and Stars

**NAME:** _____

**Directions:** Imagine you are on a trip through outer space. Draft a narrative about what you see and do on your adventure. Use the notes on page 149 to help you.

_____

_____

_____

_____

_____

_____

_____

_____

_____

**Remember!**

A strong narrative paragraph tells a story with a beginning, a middle, and an end.

# Printing Practice abc

**Directions:** Use your best printing to write two adjectives about stars.

_____     _____

**NAME:** _____

Revising
Sun, Moon, and Stars

**Directions:** Write sequence words from the Word Bank that would pair with the ones below. Then, write a sentence using a pair of the sequence words.

**Word Bank**

third    after    last    later

before _____    earlier _____

first _____    second _____

**My Sentence With Sequence Words**

_____

_____

# Time to Improve!

**Directions:** Go back to the draft you wrote on page 150. Look for places where you could add sequence words to help the reader understand the order of the story.

NAME: _____

**Directions:** Look for the series of items listed in each sentence. Use the ∧ symbol to add commas between the items.

1. The astronaut visited Mercury Venus Jupiter and Mars.

2. The alien on Mars had red hair three eyes four ears and seven arms.

3. They saw satellites planets stars and moons in space.

4. Astronauts need to bring food space suits air tanks and tools when they go in to space.

## Remember!

When you are listing several objects, you need a comma between each item.

**NAME:** _____

**Directions:** Imagine you are on a trip through outer space. Write a narrative about what you see and do on your adventure.

_____

_____

_____

_____

_____

_____

_____

_____

_____

_____

_____

_____

**NAME:** _____

**Directions:** Circle the things that you might find in a narrative about a great day.

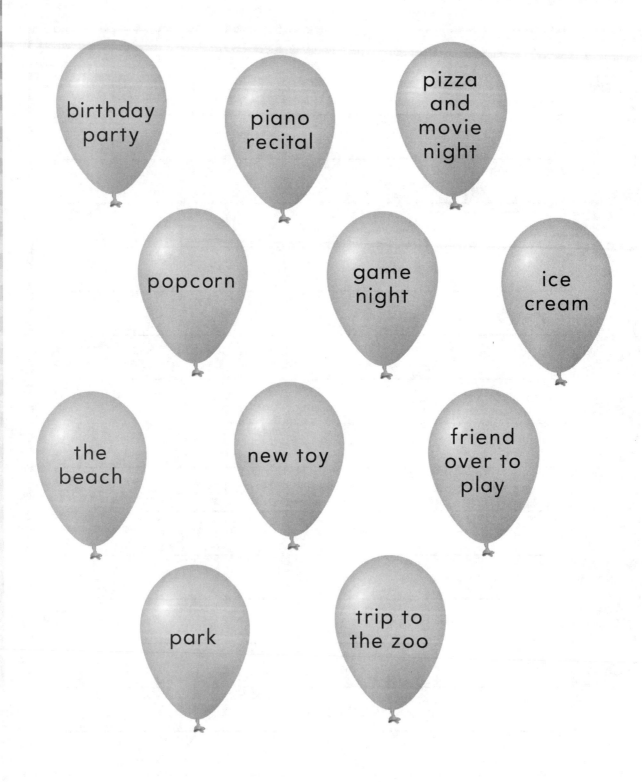

birthday party

piano recital

pizza and movie night

popcorn

game night

ice cream

the beach

new toy

friend over to play

park

trip to the zoo

**NAME:** _____

**Directions:** Read the narrative about a great day. Circle the names of people and places. Underline words that tell when events in the story are happening.

Anders was so excited when he woke up because he just knew it was going to be a great day! After dinner, the whole family was going to visit Central Park to see fireworks. Anders and his cousins, Daniel and Audrey, were going to spend the afternoon at Westbrook Zoo. The morning would continue with a trip to Cedar Beach with his cousins. Mom told Anders he could have his favorite food for breakfast, and he already smelled the pancakes cooking. They would eat a picnic lunch at the beach. Anders was certain that this would be the best day ever.

# Printing Practice abc

**Directions:** Use your best printing to write two things you think would be part of a great day.

_____   _____

**NAME:** _____

**Directions:** Write numbers on the lines to show the order in which these activities occur.

### Activity 1

_____ We get on the airplane.

_____ We drive to the airport.

_____ The plane takes off.

### Activity 2

_____ We play games and eat cake.

_____ Friends come to the party.

_____ Invitations are delivered.

### Activity 3

_____ The fireworks are fun to watch.

_____ They wait in line to buy tickets.

_____ The day is spent going on rides.

## Boost Your Learning!

Narratives should be told in a logical order. Think about the order in which things happen as you write.

NAME: _____

**Directions:** Use the ═ symbol to correct the capitalization errors.

1. mrs. cheng said that the tonka high school choir is going to perform for us today.

2. grandma nancy is taking me to westside mall to buy a new backpack and lunch box!

3. it was fun to spend the day at valleyland park with my friends luke, katrina, joel, and lauren.

4. at the zoo, ashley, eric, and jon saw animals from africa, australia, and south america.

## Boost Your Learning! 🖋

**Proper nouns,** the names of specific people and places, need to be capitalized along with the first words in sentences.

**Example:** aunt ann is taking me to grand park!

**NAME:** _____

**Directions:** Reread the narrative. Then, answer the question.

Anders was so excited when he woke up because he just knew it was going to be a great day! After dinner, the whole family was going to visit Central Park to see fireworks. Anders and his cousins, Daniel and Audrey, were going to spend the afternoon at Westbrook Zoo. The morning would continue with a trip to Cedar Beach with his cousins. Mom had told Anders he could have his favorite food for breakfast, and he already smelled the pancakes cooking. They would eat a picnic lunch at the beach. Anders was certain this would be the best day ever.

1. Does the sequence of events in the narrative make sense?

_____

_____

_____

_____

**This week I learned:** 📏✏️

- to think about the order in which events happen
- that proper nouns and first words in sentences need to be capitalized

**NAME:** _____

**Directions:** Think about what makes a day bad. Write something in each box that might make a day bad.

When you get up

_____  _____

Arriving at school

_____  _____

Lunchtime

_____  _____

After school

_____  _____

Evening

_____  _____

**Drafting**

A Bad Day

**NAME:** _____

**Directions:** Have you ever had a bad day?  Describe what happened and what you did to make the day better. Use your notes on page 159 to help you.

_____

_____

_____

_____

_____

_____

_____

_____

_____

_____

_____

> ## Remember! 
>
> A strong narrative paragraph tells a story with a beginning, a middle, and an end.

## Printing Practice  abc

**Directions:** Use your best printing to write the words *terrible*, *awful*, *horrible*, and *really bad*.

_____        _____

_____        _____

**NAME:** _____

**Directions:** Use the narrative you drafted on page 160 to complete the chart.

| A Bad Day Story | | |
|---|---|---|
| | **Event or Activity** | **Words That Tell When It Happened** |
| **First** | | |
| **Second** | | |
| **Third** | | |
| **Fourth** | | |

# Time to Improve!

**Directions:** Reread your draft on page 160. Is your story told in a logical order? Make notes to change the order of your story, if needed.

Editing

A Bad Day

**NAME:** _____

**Directions:** Use the ≡ symbol to show words that need to be capitalized.

1. daniel said, "it's a bad day when miss grant is gone and we have a substitute teacher."

2. our principal, mr. carpenter, said it was too cold to go out for recess.

3. it was a bad day because i left my permission slip for the field trip at home.

4. my brother, jim, woke up late, so we missed the bus to school.

**Remember!** ✍

Proper nouns name specific people and places.

**Time to Improve!** 🎖

**Directions:** Look at your draft on page 160. Check to make sure you capitalized the first word in each sentence and all the proper nouns.

**NAME:** _____

**Directions:** Have you ever had a bad day?  Describe what happened and what you did to make the day better.

_____

_____

_____

_____

_____

_____

_____

_____

_____

_____

_____

**Prewriting** | Ants

**NAME:** _____

**Directions:** List four places where you might see ants and four things you see ants doing. Then, write an opinion sentence telling whether or not you like ants.

## Places I See Ants

_____

_____

_____

_____

## Things Ants Do

_____

_____

_____

_____

## My Opinion About Ants

_____

_____

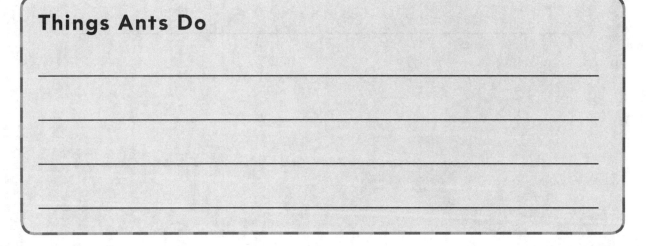

#51525—180 Days of Writing

NAME: _____

**Directions:** Read the paragraph. Underline the opinion statement. Then, circle the action words.

Many people do not like ants and want to get rid of them, but I think ants are important insects to have around. Ants help the dirt by digging tunnels in the ground. When they dig these tunnels, they move the dirt and make it healthier for young plants. Another way ants help is by eating other insects. Some insects that ants eat are dangerous to plants. Ants also help by moving seeds around. Did you know ants can carry more than 20 times their body weight? They move a lot of seeds that way and take them to places that make it easier for the seeds to grow. Even though ants are not fun around food and picnics, they provide great help to the earth!

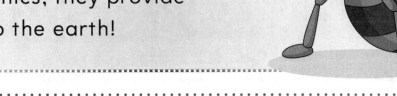

# Printing Practice abc

**Directions:** Use your best printing to write *soldier ants* and *carpenter ants*.

_____

_____

**NAME:** _____

**Directions:** Draw a line to match each sentence on the left with the opinion it best supports on the right.

Ants eat insects that harm plants.

Ants can cause damage to wood.

Some ants bite people.

Ants move soil, and that helps plants grow.

Ants move into people's homes looking for food and water.

Ants carry seeds, which helps plants grow in new areas.

**Opinion #1**
Many people do not like to see ants.

**Opinion #2**
Ants are insects that help the earth.

**Boost Your Learning!**

When writing an opinion paragraph, first introduce your topic, and then state your opinion by telling what you think.

**NAME:** _____

**Directions:** Find words that are repeated in the sentences. Use the $\mathcal{l}$ symbol to show any words you want to remove.

1. The ant crawls crawls up the wall.

2. Ants can eat eat the eggs of many insects.

3. When ants carry carry seeds, they take them to new places to grow.

4. Tunnel ants dig dig and move the dirt, and this helps plants.

## Boost Your Learning! 🚀

Check your writing carefully to be sure you do not repeat words.

**Example:** Ants eat ~~eat~~ many insects.

**NAME:** _____

**Directions:** Revisit the opinion paragraph. Underline sentences that support the author's opinion.

Many people do not like ants and want to get rid of them, but I think ants are important insects to have around. Ants help the dirt by digging tunnels in the ground. When they dig these tunnels, they move the dirt and make it healthier and better for growing plants. Another way ants help is by eating other insects. Some insects that ants eat are dangerous to plants. Ants also help by moving seeds around. Did you know ants can carry more than 20 times their body weight? They move a lot of seeds that way and take them to places that make it easier for the seeds to grow. Even though ants are not fun around food and picnics, they provide great help to the earth!

## This week I learned: 🖊🖌

- how to start an opinion paragraph with an opinion statement
- to delete repeated verbs and insert new ones

**NAME:** _____

**Directions:** Read the statement. Decide whether each fact agrees or disagrees with the statement. Then, place the them in the correct columns.

### Statement

Bees are pests and are not good for anything.

### Bee Facts

Bees make honey, and many people like to eat honey.

Bees sting people, and that hurts.

Many people are allergic to bee stings.

Bees pollinate plants, and that helps them to grow.

Bees make loud, annoying, buzzing sounds.

| Agree | Disagree |
|---|---|
|  |  |

Drafting Bees

**NAME:** _____

**Directions:** Do you think bees are useful? Explain your answer and give supporting details. Use your notes from page 169 to help you.

_____

_____

_____

_____

_____

_____

_____

_____

_____

_____

> ## Remember!
>
> A strong opinion paragraph:
>
> • has an introductory and a concluding sentence stating your opinion
>
> • gives reasons that support the opinion

## Printing Practice abc

**Directions:** Use your best printing to write the three kinds of bees: *queens*, *workers*, and *drones*.

_____    _____

_____

Revising

Bees

**NAME:** _____

**Directions:** Write an opinion statement to go with each introductory sentence.

**1.** Bees are insects, so they have six legs.

_____

_____

**2.** Honey is produced by bees in their hives.

_____

_____

**3.** Pollen is spread by bees, and this helps plants to grow.

_____

_____

## Time to Improve!

**Directions:** Reread the opinion paragraph you drafted on page 170. Did you write an introduction sentence and an opinion statement? Add the sentences if you need to.

Editing  Bees

**NAME:** _____

**Directions:** Read the facts.  Then, rewrite them to make them opinions.

**1.** Bees can sting people.

_____

_____

**2.** Bees make honey.

_____

_____

**3.** Bees are black, yellow, and fuzzy.

_____

_____

## Time to Improve!

**Directions:** Review the paragraph you wrote on page 170.  Look for words that show which sentences are opinions.  Add opinion statements to sentences that need them.

**NAME:** _____

**Directions:** Do you think bees are useful? Explain your answer and give supporting details.

_____

_____

_____

_____

_____

_____

_____

_____

_____

_____

_____

_____

**Prewriting**
In the Wind

**NAME:** _____

**Directions:** Place check marks in the bubbles with things that could be moved by a light wind. Place stars in the bubbles with things that could be moved by a strong wind.

bubbles

kite

car

leaf

boat

paper

windmill

feather

rock

balloon

tree branches

marble

**NAME:** _____

**Directions:** Read the paragraph. Underline the topic and conclusion sentences. Draw lines through sentences that do not stay on topic.

Wind cannot be seen, but it is easy to see what wind does. Sometimes, the weather is sunny. Wind makes things move. It takes different types of wind to move different objects. When you blow air out of your mouth, you are making a little wind. You can blow through a straw and make a feather move. It is fun to find feathers birds have lost. The harder you blow, the farther you can move it. Wind from a fan can make the feather move even farther. You can see that it is windy outdoors when tree branches move. This kind of wind helps move kites up into the sky. Kites have many colorful designs and are pretty to see. On a windy day, you can see papers and leaves moving in the wind. Even though you cannot see the wind, if you watch carefully, you know where it is.

# Printing Practice abc

**Directions:** Use your best printing to write a sentence about what the wind can do.

_____

_____

Revising

In the Wind

**NAME:** _____

**Directions:** Read the original sentence. Write a list of adjectives to describe wind. Then, list things that the wind moves. Use your adjectives to create a new sentence.

**Original Sentence**
The wind blows.

**Adjectives about the Wind**

_____        _____

_____        _____

**Things the Wind Moves**

_____        _____

_____        _____

**My New and Improved Sentence**

_____

_____

_____

**Boost Your Learning!** 🚀

Help your writing come alive by using adjectives and giving specific examples.

**NAME:** _____

**Directions:** Read the lists of words. Find the words that do not belong. Use the  symbol to delete them. Then, select one list and write a sentence using only the words that are about the same topic.

1. air flow, breeze, heat, strong winds, rain shower

2. kite, fly, rock, soar, burn

3. sail, horse, canoe, bike, raft

4. radio, fan, windmill, map, weather vane

**My Topic Sentence:**

_____

_____

_____

**Remember!**

When you are writing, your ideas should be about the same topic. Delete words or sentences that are off topic.

**NAME:** _____

**Directions:** Read the paragraph.  Then, answer the question.

Wind cannot be seen, but it is easy to see what wind does.  Wind makes things move.  It takes different types of wind to move different objects.  When you blow air out of your mouth, you make a little wind.  You can blow through a straw and make a feather move.  The harder you blow, the farther you can move it.  Wind from a fan can make the feather move even farther.  You can see that it is windy outdoors when tree branches move.  This kind of wind helps move kites up into the sky.  On a windy day, you can see papers and leaves moving in the wind.  Even though you cannot see the wind, you know where it is.

**1.** Does the author stay on topic?  How do you know?

_____

_____

NAME: _____

**Directions:** Brainstorm objects that can be pushed or pulled. An example is provided.

grocery cart

Things that are Pushed or Pulled

Drafting

Push or Pull

NAME: _____

**Directions:** Describe how objects are pushed or pulled. Include differences between pulling and pushing. Use your notes on page 179 to help you.

_____

_____

_____

_____

_____

_____

_____

_____

_____

_____

_____

> ## Remember!
>
> A strong informative paragraph includes:
>
> - an introductory and a concluding sentence
>
> - details that support the main idea

# Printing Practice abc

**Directions:** Use your best printing to write one sentence about something that can be pushed or pulled.

_____

_____

_____

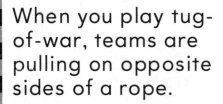

**NAME:** _____

**Directions:** Match the sentences on the left with the sentences on the right that have the same topic.

| | |
|---|---|
| When you play tug-of-war, teams are pulling on opposite sides of a rope. | A stroller moves quickly if you are running while you push it. |
| When you walk and push a stroller, the stroller moves slowly. | If you are outside a car, you open the door by pulling on it. |
| When you shoot a basketball, you are pushing it. | Tug-of-war is a good example of using a strong force to pull. |
| If you are inside a car, you push the door to open it. | Soccer players push the ball as they kick it down the field. |

# Time to Improve!

**Directions:** Reread your draft on page 180. Check and see if all the detail sentences match your topic and conclusion sentences.

NAME: _____

Editing

Push or Pull

**Directions:** Some pronouns in the sentences are not correct. Use the ✍ symbol to delete them, and write the correct words above them.

1. If you walk slowly while pulling a wagon, they will move slowly.

2. When you hit a baseball with a bat, you are really pushing them.

3. The children pushed his race cars down the track.

4. A boat moves when the wind pushes against their sails.

## Time to Improve!

**Directions:** Reread the paragraph on page 180. Check and see if all the words in your sentences make sense.

NAME: _____

**Directions:** Describe how objects are pushed or pulled. Include differences between pulling and pushing.

_____

_____

_____

_____

_____

_____

_____

_____

**NAME:** _____

**Directions:** List at least three reasons why you should or should not spend your time doing these activities.

## Reading a Book

## Watching Television

WEEK 35
DAY
2

**NAME:** _____

Drafting
Watching TV or Reading?

**Directions:** Read the paragraph. Draw lines through phrases that are repeated.

It is fun to have free time, but deciding what to do can be difficult. I think it is better to spend free time reading books. When you read books, you learn things. You can learn about people, places, and animals all over the world. You can learn about how things grow and how things work. When you read books, you can imagine. You can imagine you are the character in the story and that you are experiencing the same things the character is. When you read books, you get better at reading. You get better at recognizing words, reading words correctly, and understanding new words. When you have free time, you really should choose to read a book.

# Printing Practice abc

**Directions:** Use your best printing to complete the sentences.

My favorite book is _____.

My favorite TV show is _____.

© Shell Education                    #51525—180 Days of Writing                    185

**NAME:** _____

**Directions:** Read each fact. Change the fact to an opinion statement. Write your new opinion sentences on the lines.

1. You can learn by watching shows about history on television.

_____

_____

_____

2. Parents and teachers tell children to read.

_____

_____

_____

3. The library is one place you can go to get books to read.

_____

_____

_____

**Boost Your Learning!** 🚀

When you write opinion statements, use words to show that they are your opinion.

**NAME:** _____

**Directions:** Use the ⟲ symbol to remove the repeated words in the second sentences.  Write new words in their places.

1. Many people think that children should spend time reading books.  Many people think that reading is good for children.

    _____

    _____

    _____

2. Everyone should spend some time at the library during the summer.  Everyone should read at least ten books in the summer.

    _____

    _____

    _____

**Boost Your Learning!** 🚀

Sentences need a variety of beginnings. Replace repeated words with different words to make sentences more interesting.

Publishing

Watching TV or Reading?

**NAME:** _____

**Directions:** Revisit the opinion paragraph. Underline phrases that are repeated. Use the ∧ symbol to replace the repeated words.

It is fun to have free time, but deciding what to do can be difficult. I think it is better to spend free time reading books. When you read books, you can learn. You can learn about people, places, and animals all over the world. You can learn about how things grow and how things work. When you read books, you can imagine. You can imagine you are the character in the story and that you are experiencing the same things the character is. When you read books, you get better at reading. You get better at recognizing words, reading words correctly, and understanding new words. When you have free time, you really should choose to read a book.

## This week I learned: 🖊️📓

- to provide statements that support my opinion
- how to change sentences so they have different beginnings

**NAME:** _____

**Directions:** List at least three ideas in each column.

## The Beach

| What I Like | What I Don't Like |
|---|---|
|  |  |

## The Park

| What I Like | What I Don't Like |
|---|---|
|  |  |

Drafting

Beach or Park?

**NAME:** _____

**Directions:** Do you prefer the beach or the park? Explain why using strong supporting details. Use your notes on page 189 to help you.

_____

_____

_____

_____

_____

_____

_____

_____

_____

_____

> ## Remember!
>
> A strong opinion paragraph includes:
>
> - an introductory sentence that states your opinion
>
> - details to support your ideas
>
> - a concluding sentence

## Printing Practice abc

**Directions:** Use your best printing to write the names of two beaches or two parks you like to visit.

_____

_____

**NAME:** _____

**Directions:** Read the facts. Revise the sentences by adding words to make them opinions. Write your new sentences on the lines.

**1.** There are many things to do at the beach such as swimming, building sandcastles, and playing games.

_____

_____

_____

**2.** At a park, you can exercise by climbing, swinging, running, and jumping.

_____

_____

_____

**3.** Beaches are busy places in the summer, and many people spend time there.

_____

_____

_____

## Time to Improve! 🎖

**Directions:** Reread the paragraph you wrote on page 190. Find places where you need to add opinion statements.

**Editing**
Beach or Park?

**NAME:** _____

**Directions:** Read the sentences. Use the ⟲ symbol to remove words that have been repeated.

1. I think the beach is the best place to go in the summer, I think.

2. Everyone needs to spend time at the park the park to get exercise and have fun.

3. The best thing about going to the beach is getting ice cream on the way home, that's the best thing.

4. The park near my house is the greatest greatest park of all.

## Time to Improve! ✦

**Directions:** Reread your paragraph on page 190. Check to see if your sentences start in a variety of ways. Change sentences that have repetitive beginnings.

**NAME:** _____

**Directions:** Do you prefer the beach or the park? Explain why using strong supporting details.

_____

_____

_____

_____

_____

_____

_____

_____

_____

_____

_____

_____

_____

# ANSWER KEY

The activity pages that do not have specific answers to them are not included in this answer key. Students' answers will vary on these activity pages, so check that students are staying on task.

## Week 1: Rules at School

### Day 1 (page 14)

Students should check marks next to the following rules: 1. Be on time for class; 2. Listen to your teacher; 3. Keep your hands and feet to yourself; 5. Take good care of classroom materials; 7. Walk at school.; 8. Be kind to your classmates; and 10. Always do your best.

### Day 2 (page 15)

Underlined parts should include: Today our class decided we should have class rules that we would all follow. Mrs. Wright gave us three sheets of paper and asked us to write a classroom rule on each page. Our class looked at the rules we had written and found many that were the same. We chose five rules for our class to follow this year.

### Day 3 (page 16)

The sentences should be in the following order: Every classroom needs rules. First, we decide we should have rules. Then, we think about which rules we should have. Finally, we follow the rules we create. This way, our classroom will be a safe environment.

### Day 4 (page 17)

1. My sister attends **Abraham Lincoln** Preschool and has to follow the rules.
2. Our teacher, **Mrs. Gillespie**, has worked hard to set up rules at **Park Heights School**.
3. **Mr**. Bolander allows his class to set up their own classroom rules.
4. **Mrs**. Eddy reminds her students how helpful rules can be.

### Day 5 (page 18)

**It** was a great first day of school. **I** am in second grade at **Elliot Grove Elementary School**. **My** teacher is **Mrs**. **Wright**. **Today**, our class decided we should have class rules that we would all follow. **Then**, **Mrs**. **Wright** gave each of us three sheets of paper and asked us to write a classoom rule on each one. **Our** class looked at the rules we had written and found many that were the same. **We** chose five rules for our class to follow this year. **I** know it is going to be a good year!

## Week 2: Friends at School

### Day 4 (page 22)

1. It is fun to play with my friends **Amir**, **Lily**, and **Aisha**.
2. We are all in second grade at **Fern Hill Elementary School**.
3. My mom drives me to **Paul Revere Park** to play with my friend, **Gabe**.
4. **Ariel's** little sister likes to play with us at the park, too.

### Day 5 (page 23)

See the Narrative Writing Rubric on page 204.

## Week 3: In the City

### Day 2 (page 25)

Students should underline the following: A city has many parks where children can play. People can do many things in a city, such as go to a zoo or a museum. Cities are busy places. There is almost always something happening in a city.

## Week 4: In the Country

### Day 1 (page 29)

The following should be checked: barn, pigpen, cow, horse, and haystack

### Day 5 (page 33)

See Informative/Explanatory Writing Rubric on page 203.

## Week 5: Why Eat Apples

### Day 1 (page 34)

The following should be check marked: Apples help make your heart strong; Apples help you exercise; Apples are healthy fruits; Apples contain vitamins; Apples can keep you from getting sick.

### Day 2 (page 35)

**Everyone should eat apples every day.** Apples are colorful and crunchy. Apples are healthy snacks. They have vitamins that help keep you from getting sick. Apples are delicious. Eating apples can make your heart strong. **It is a good idea to eat an apple every day**.

### Day 3 (page 36)

The following should be crossed out: I had a banana for breakfast. Apples come in many different colors. My mom gave me crackers.

### Day 4 (page 37)

**Singular**: tree, basket, heart
**Plural**: apples, leaves, stems

### Day 5 (page 38)

1. The author thinks apples are good for you. The author says that people should "eat apples everyday" and that apples are a "healthy" and "delicious snack."
2. The author could have used different adjectives that are more descriptive.

# ANSWER KEY *(cont.)*

## Week 6: How to Eat Apples

### Day 3 (page 41)

Students should cross out the following: Apples are great snacks because there are so many ways they can be eaten. Do you like baked potatoes? Apple pies, apple cake, and applesauce are good treats.

### Day 4 (page 42)

apples, pies, sauces, caramels, slices, cakes, fruits, seeds, cores, stems, trees

### Day 5 (page 43)

See the Opinion Writing Rubric on page 202.

## Week 7: Rain Forests

### Day 1 (page 44)

The following should have *X*'s: swimming pools; grocery stores; school buses; libraries; apartment buildings

### Day 3 (page 46)

1. Suggestion to replace *see*: view, look at
2. Suggestion to replace *hear*: listen to
3. Suggestion to replace *smell*: scent, odor

### Day 4 (page 47)

Words that should be circled and written correctly (in order as they appear):

diferent/different; animols/animals; rainforrests/rainforests; viry/very; grond/ground; froogs/frogs

## Week 8: Temperate Forests

### Day 1 (page 49)

Students should place check marks next to the following: 1. Many people live near temperate forests; 3. Temperate forests have four seasons; 5. Good soil for growing plants can be found in temperate forests; 6. Temperate forests usually get lots of rain; 7. Some people live in cabins in temperate forests.

### Day 3 (page 51)

forest—woods

path— route

stream—creek

cottage—cabin

### Day 4 (page 52)

Words that should be circled and written correctly (in order as they appear): forrest—forest; anemals—animals; smel—smell; weads—weeds.

### Day 5 (page 53)

See Informative/Explanatory Writing Rubric on page 203.

## Week 9: Jack-o-Lanterns

### Day 2 (page 55)

Students should underline the following sentences: I started with a big pumpkin, and everyone knows that big pumpkins are scarier than small pumpkins. Those pointy teeth look scary. I think my jack-o-lantern is the scariest of all.

### Day 4 (page 57).

1. They went to the **pumpkin patch** to get a pumpkin to carve for Halloween.
2. Be sure your jack-o lantern is carved and ready by **October 31**.
3. You might want to have an adult help cut your jack-o-lanterns because knives are usually **sharp**.
4. People are usually very **frightened** when they see a scary jack-o-lantern.

### Day 5 (page 58)

1. The author gives details such as "The jack-o-lantern I carved is scary," and "Those pointy teeth look scary."

## Week 10: Scarecrows

### Day 3 (page 61)

Sentences that do *not* make sense include: Scarecrows are often seen in on when the fall. Birds usually fly up to away from scarecrows. The arms and legs of with scarecrows wave when the wind blows.

### Day 5 (page 63)

See Opinion Writing Rubric on page 202.

# ANSWER KEY *(cont.)*

## Week 11: Being Thankful

**Day 1** (page 64)

Leaves that should be check marked: You will feel good if you give thanks; People give thanks for many things; You should always be thankful for those around you; When people do things for you, you should thank them.

**Day 2** (page 65)

Students should circle the following sentences:

People usually feel better when they are thankful. When you find a reason to be thankful, it can help you feel good.

Students should underline the following sentences:

You will feel better when you are thankful you have food. If you are thankful you can learn, you will feel better. Instead of thinking your clothes are too old, be happy you have clothes and you will feel better.

**Day 3** (page 66)

you are—you're
you will—you'll
you have—you've
will not—won't
where is—where's
it is—it's

**Day 4** (page 67)

Students should add spaces between the following words:

1. remember the; good things
2. many things; feel thankful
3. Answers will vary.

**Day 5** (page 68)

they are—they're; do not–don't; you are—you're; you will—you'll; you are—you're; you are—you're; you will—you'll; you will—you'll

## Week 12: Sharing Thanks

**Day 3** (page 71)

**Contractions:** they're, she's, wouldn't, I'll, can't, that's

**First Word:** they; she; would; I; can; that

**Second Word:** are; is; not; will; not; is

**Day 4** (page 72)

1. People **can share** thanks by writing **a thankful** note.
2. Delivering a plate of cookies **is a** good way to **share thanks**.
3. Saying "thank you" is another **way of** sharing thanks.
4. It is important **to share** thanks when someone **has helped** you.
5. When **we show** we are thankful, we feel **good inside**.

**Day 5** (page 73)

See Opinion Writing Rubric on page 202.

## Week 13: Thunderstorms

**Day 1** (page 74)

Students should check mark the following:

thunder; fallen trees; lightning; tornadoes; flooding

**Day 2** (page 75)

**Thunderstorms can be scary and dangerous.** It is best to stay inside during a storm. <u>Heavy rain during a thunderstorm can cause rivers, streams, and lakes to flood.</u> It can be very windy during a thunderstorm. <u>The wind might make trees fall and cause branches to blow around.</u> Thunder is very loud. Loud noises are often frightening. <u>Lightning can strike during a storm, and you don't want to be around that.</u> Be sure to stay indoors during thunderstorms to be safe.

**Day 3** (page 76)

People get very scared during thunderstorms—These are the reasons thunderstorms scare people.

Thunderstorms can be dangerous at times—If you are careful, you can avoid the dangers of thunderstorms.

Thunderstorms create loud noises—If you listen carefully, the sounds will tell you what is happening.

**Day 4** (page 77)

1. **When** you see lightning, **you** know you **will** soon hear thunder.
2. It can rain **very** hard in the middle **of** a thunderstorm.
3. **When** lightning flashes it **makes** the sky light up.
4. Hail is ice **that** falls **from** the sky during a thunderstorm.

## Week 14: Snowstorms

**Day 1** (page 79)

The following should be check marked: blowing snow, slippery roads, cold temperatures, hard to see outside, snow to shovel, howling winds, school is closed

**Day 4** (page 82)

1. We **were** going to have hot cocoa after sledding.
2. The snow is so **quiet** when it falls, it does not make a sound.
3. Look over **there** and see the snowman they made.
4. She got a new hat **from** her grandmother.
5. Our school **often** closes because of bad weather.
6. Would anyone like **another** cookie?

**Day 5** (page 83)

See Informative/Explanatory Rubric on page 203.

# ANSWER KEY *(cont.)*

## Week 15: Gifts to Me

**Day 2** (page 85)

My mom said my sister was so **happy** when she brought the book home and wrapped it. On the day of the party, my sister was **anxious** to give me my gift. As I opened the gift, my sister was **smiling**, **laughing**, and **jumping up and down**. I **loved** the gift, and I loved seeing my sister so **happy**, **excited**, and **joyful**.

**Day 4** (page 87)

1. I usually get presents on my birthday**,** at Christmas**,** and for Valentine's Day
2. We get hats**,** scarves**,** and mittens for winter.
3. My brother had a hockey stick**,** ice skates**,** and a sled on his gift list.
4. My dog got bones**,** squeaky toys**,** and treats on his birthday.
5. Our teacher receives notes**,** pictures**,** and hugs at school.

**Day 5** (Page 88)

1. The author does a good job of using the feeling words, "smiling, laughing, and jumping" and "happy, excited, and joyful."

## Week 16: Giving to Others

**Day 3** (page 91)

**Happy:** cheerful; joyful; pleased; contented; glad

**Excited:** eager; anxious; thrilled; enthusiastic; energized

**Thankful:** grateful; satisfied

**Day 4** (page 92)

1. My friend got games**,** puzzles**,** and books for her birthday.
2. We need to prepare invitations**,** snacks**,** and games for the party.
3. My grandma says the best gifts are hugs**,** smiles**,** and cuddles.
4. I can't wait to give gifts to my friend**,** my dad**,** and my sister.

**Day 5** (page 93)

See Narrative Writing Rubric on page 204.

## Week 17: Building Snowmen

**Day 1** (page 94)

1. snowballs
2. stick
3. carrot
4. hat
5. scarf
6. button

**Day 2** (page 95)

1. It was a great day to build a snowman. 2. We bundled up and hurried outside to get started. 3. We rolled a big snowball and set it in the middle of our yard. 4. We rolled a medium-size snowball and set it on top of the large snowball. 5. We rolled a small snowball for the snowman's head. 6. We got a carrot and some large buttons from my mom and used them to make a nose, eyes, and mouth. 7. We got sticks for arms and an old hat and scarf.

**Day 4** (page 97)

We spent a lot of time playing outside. When we came in, we were hungry and wanted a snack. **First** we took off our snow clothes and hung them up to dry. **Second** we looked in the cupboard for a snack. **Third** we decided to make hot cocoa. **Fourth** we poured milk into a mug. The **fifth** thing we did was heat the milk. Our **sixth** job was to stir the cocoa powder into the warm milk. Marshmallows were added **seventh**. **Eighth** we enjoyed a yummy cup of cocoa.

**Day 5** (page 98)

It is a strong narrative because it is descriptive and told in order.

## Week 18: Sledding

**Day 4** (page 102)

1. **First**, I brushed my teeth.
2. **Then**, my sister made us breakfast.
3. **After**, we put on warm clothes
4. **Next**, we went to the park.
5. **Finally**, we had fun sledding.

**Day 5** (page 103)

See Narrative Writing Rubric on page 204.

## Week 19: Zebras

**Day 1** (page 104)

The following statements should be check marked: Zebras live in Africa; Each zebra has a different stripe pattern; Young zebras are foals; A group of zebras is called a herd; Zebras are herbivores; they eat plants, Zebras are closely related to horses and donkeys.

**Day 2** (page 105)

Students should cross out the following sentences: It is very hot and dry in Africa; Baby goats can stand just hours after they are born; Giraffes have very long necks.

**Day 4** (page 107)

Words that should be crossed out:

1. houses, airports
2. crayons, lions
3. horse, book
4. pizza, bus
5. computers, pencils

**Day 5** (page 108)

1. No; there is a sentence about baby goats and a sentence, about giraffes' necks even though the paragraph is about zebras.

© Shell Education

#51525—180 Days of Writing

197

# ANSWER KEY (cont.)

## Week 20: Penguins

### Day 1 (page 109)

The following should be check marked: Penguins live where it is very cold, You can find penguins in the water but not in the sky, Penguins can swim but they cannot fly, Each set of penguins has one or two babies a year.

### Day 4 (page 112)

1. Penguins can be **quite playful**.
2. Penguins spend time **in the** water and on land.
3. Father penguins care **for eggs** during the winter.
4. Baby penguins stay **with their** parents for about six months.

### Day 5 (page 113)

See Informative/Explanatory Rubric on page 203.

## Week 21: Important People

### Day 1 (page 114)

Thomas Edison—inventor of the motion-picture camera and electric lightbulb

Amelia Earhart—first female pilot to fly alone across the Atlantic Ocean

Abraham Lincoln—16th president of the United States; he helped get rid of slavery

Ruby Bridges—first African American child in Louisiana to attend an all-white school

### Day 2 (page 115)

**Everyone should learn more about these great Americans.** These are some of the greatest. Thomas Edison was an inventor. He invented many things. Amelia Earhart was a pilot who loved to fly. Abraham Lincoln fought to make life better for all American people. Ruby Bridges was brave when she helped change schools. These important people and the things they did are worth knowing about.

### Day 3 (page 116)

F; Helen Keller learned to communicate even though she was blind and deaf.

O; I think Martin Luther King Jr. was a great American.

O; The best thing about George Washington is that he was the first president.

F; Martin Luther King Jr. helped change the way people were treated.

F; Sally Ride was the first American woman to travel in space.

## Week 22: Important Places

### Day 3 (page 121)

1. **I prefer** going to the zoo in our city.
2. **I think the best** place to visit is Boston, MA.
3. **The best thing** about my town is the carnival we have every year.
4. Everyone **should** take a vacation to California.
5. **It is better** to go to Washington, D.C., than Florida.

### Day 4 (page 122)

1. Our favorite building in **Washington**, D.C., is the **Washington Memorial**.
2. We thought the **Old North Church** was the most interesting place to see in **Boston**.
3. The giant sequoia trees in **Yosemite National Park** are fun to see.
4. My family thinks our trip to the **Grand Canyon** was our best one ever.
5. Everyone should go to the **Alamo** in **Texas**.
6. My favorite vacation was to Mount Rushmore.

### Day 5 (page 123)

See Opinion Writing Rubric on page 202.

## Week 23: Little Red Riding Hood

### Day 1 (page 124)

The following words in each section should be circled: **Setting:** forest or woods; **Characters:** grandmother, mother, hunter, little girl, wolf; **Props:** red hood, basket, food, flowers

### Day 2 (page 125)

Students should underline the following sentences:

There is a girl called Little Red Hoodie because she wears red hoodies every day. One afternoon, her mother says, "Please take this dinner over to your grandmother." As she rides her bike towards her grandmother's house, she meets a woman. "What is in your basket?" the woman asks. Little Red Hoodie says, "It's dinner for my grandmother." The lady asks where her grandmother lives, Little Red Hoodie tells her and they go on their way. Little Red Hoodie arrives at the house and sees the woman she met on the way. Little Red Hoodie says, "Where is my grandma?" The woman tells her, "Your grandma left and told me to eat her dinner." Little Red Hoodie hears a noise from the other room, opens the door, and sees her grandmother resting in bed. Little Red Hoodie was very confused.

### Day 4 (page 127)

1. The old woman said, "I am going to catch that runaway cookie!"
2. "We are looking for someone to help us make bread," said the animals.

The following use quotation marks correctly: Goldilocks says, "This chair is too soft."; The prince asked, "Who is the owner of this glass slipper?"

# ANSWER KEY (cont.)

## Week 24: Goldilocks and the Three Bears

**Day 4** (page 132)

**Answer:** Jordan told me, "My favorite fairy tale is *The Gingerbread Man*."

**Answer:** "I think Goldilocks is cold, so she goes into the bears' house to get warm," answered Emily.

**Answer:** Cally said, "I think the three bears should let Goldilocks finish her nap, and give her a snack."

**Day 5** (page 133)

See Narrative Writing Rubric on page 204.

## Week 25: Frogs

**Day 1** (page 134)

The following should be check marked: Tree frogs have pads on their feet. Frogs have large eyes. Frogs are shades of green. Frogs that live in water have webbed feet. Some frogs have spotted skin.

**Day 2** (page 135)

Not all frogs look the same. <u>Frogs can be many different colors.</u> <u>Some frogs are green or brown to blend in with their surroundings.</u> Frogs begin their lives as tadpoles. <u>Poison dart frogs are colorful to let predators know to stay away.</u> Frogs range in size from less than one inch (2.54 centimeters) to more than 12 inches (30 centimeters) long. There are many endangered frogs in the world. <u>Most frogs have big eyes that let them see all around.</u> Some people think that a frog will turn into a prince when it is kissed. <u>Frogs have different types of feet.</u> <u>Webbed feet help frogs living in water swim.</u> <u>Pads on their fingers and toes help tree frogs climb.</u> The different appearances make frogs interesting to see.

**Day 4** (page 137)

1. Strong back **legs** and **webbed** feet **help** frogs swim.
2. Humans are **helped** by frogs because **frogs** eat **insects**.
3. Each species of frog **makes** its own **special** sound.
4. Tadpoles go **through** several **stages** before they are **adult** frogs.
5. Pads on their fingers and toes help **tree frogs** climb.

**Day 5** (page 138)

1. No; the sentences are all about frogs, but not all are about what they look like.

## Week 26: Turtles

**Day 1** (page 139)

The following should be circled: Turtles are reptiles, Turtles have upper and lower shells, Turtles are cold blooded, Turtles lay eggs, Some turtles live on land and others in water, Turtle shells have different designs.

**Day 4** (page 142)

1. The **sea turtles** live in the Pacific Ocean.
2. The children searched for turtles at the **beach**.
3. My **sister** is doing a research report on turtles for her class at **school**.
4. On Tuesday, we are going on a **field trip** to an **aquarium**.

**Day 5** (page 143)

See Informative/Explanatory Writing Rubric on page 203.

## Week 27: Planets

**Day 1** (page 144)

Words that should be check marked: astronaut, Mars, Jupiter, Saturn, alien, Mercury, rocket, Venus

**Day 2** (page 145)

An **astronaut** decided to take a trip to the <u>planets</u>. He blasted off from <u>Earth</u> in his rocket and shot up into the sky. The **astronaut** stopped at <u>Mercury</u> and found it was close to the sun and was too hot. So he went on. On <u>Venus</u>, he met a nice **alien**. They became friends and decided to travel together. The **astronaut** and **alien** skipped over Earth and visited <u>Mars</u> and then <u>Jupiter</u>. They spent a long time exploring the big red spot on <u>Jupiter</u> and tried to walk around it. The rings of Saturn confused the friends, so they went on to see <u>Uranus</u> and <u>Neptune</u>. After <u>Neptune</u>, they were both tired, so the **astronaut** took the **alien** back to <u>Venus</u> before heading home to <u>Earth</u>.

## Week 28: Sun, Moon, and Stars

**Day 3** (page 151)

Sequence Pairs: before/after; earlier/later; first/last; second/third

**Day 4** (page 152)

1. The astronaut visited Mercury, Venus, Jupiter, and Mars.
2. The alien on Mars had red hair, three eyes, four ears, and seven arms.
3. They saw satellites, planets, stars, and moons in space.
4. Astronauts need to bring food, space suits, air tanks, and tools when they go in to space.

**Day 5** (page 153)

See Narrative Writing Rubric on page 204.

# ANSWER KEY (cont.)

## Week 29: A Great Day

**Day 2** (page 155)

**Anders** was so excited <u>when he woke up</u>, because he just knew it was going to be a great day! <u>After dinner</u>, the whole family was going to visit **Central Park** to see fireworks. **Anders** and his cousins, **Daniel** and **Audrey**, were going to spend the <u>afternoon</u> at **Westbrook Zoo**. The <u>morning</u> would continue with a trip to **Cedar Beach** with his cousins. **Mom** told **Anders** he could have his favorite food for <u>breakfast</u>, and he already smelled the pancakes cooking. They would eat a picnic <u>lunch</u> at the beach. **Anders** was certain that this would be the best day ever.

**Day 3** (page 156)

**Activity 1:** 2. We get on the airplane. 1. We drive to the airport. 3. The plane takes off.

**Activity 2:** 3. We play games and eat cake; 2. Friends come to the party; 1. Invitations are delivered

**Activity 3:** 3. The fireworks are fun to watch. 1. They wait in line to buy tickets. 2. The day is spent going on rides.

**Day 4** (page 157)
1. **Mrs. Cheng** said that the **Tonka High School** choir is going to perform for us today.
2. **Grandma Nancy** is taking me to **Westside Mall** to buy a new backpack and lunch box!
3. **It** was fun to spend the day at **Valleyland Park** with my friends **Luke**, **Katrina**, **Joel**, and **Lauren**.
4. **At** the zoo, **Ashley**, **Eric**, and **Jon** saw animals from **Africa**, **Australia**, and **South America**.

**Day 5** (page 158)

No; the sequence is out of order and does not make sense.

## Week 30: A Bad Day

**Day 4** (page 162)
1. **Daniel** said, "**It's** a bad day when **Miss Grant** is gone and we have a substitute teacher."
2. **Our** principal, **Mr. Carpenter**, said it was too cold to go out for recess.
3. **It** was a bad day because **I** left my permission slip for the field trip at home.
4. **My** brother, **Jim**, woke up late so we missed the bus to school.

**Day 5** (page 163)

See Narrative Writing Rubric on page 204.

## Week 31: Ants

**Day 2** (page 165)

Many people do not **like** ants and want to **get** rid of them, but <u>I</u> **think** <u>ants are important insects to have around</u>. Ants **help** the dirt by **digging** tunnels in the ground. When they **dig** these tunnels they **move** the dirt and **make** it healthier for young plants. Another way ants help is by **eating** other insects. Some insects that ants **eat** are dangerous to plants. Ants also help by **moving** seeds around. Did you know ants can **carry** more than 20 times their body weight? They **move** a lot of seeds that way and **take** them to places that **make** it easier for the seeds to **grow**. Even though ants are not fun around food and picnics, they **provide** great help to the earth!

**Day 3** (page 166)

**Opinion #1:** Ants can cause damage to wood; Some ants bite people; Ants move into people's homes looking for food and water.
**Opinion #2:** Ants eat insects that harm plants; Ants move soil, and that helps plants grow; Ants carry seeds, which helps plants grow in new areas.

**Day 4** (page 167)
1. The ant crawls ~~crawls~~ up the wall.
2. Ants can eat ~~eat~~ the eggs of many insects.
3. When ants carry ~~carry~~ seeds, they take them to new places to grow.
4. Tunnel ants dig ~~dig~~ and move the dirt, and this helps plants.

**Day 5** (page 168)

Many people do not like ants and want to get rid of them, but I think ants are important insects to have around. <u>Ants help the dirt by digging tunnels in the ground.</u> <u>When they dig these tunnels they move the dirt and make it healthier for young plants.</u> <u>Another way ants help is by eating other insects.</u> Some insects that ants eat are dangerous to plants. <u>Ants also help by moving seeds around.</u> Did you know ants can carry more than 20 times their body weight? <u>They move a lot of seeds that way and take them to places that make it easier for the seeds to grow.</u> Even though ants are not fun around food and picnics, they provide great help to the earth!

## Week 32: Bees

**Day 1** (page 169)

**Agree:** Bees sting people and that hurts; Many people are allergic to bee stings; Bees make loud, annoying, buzzing sounds.

**Disagree:** Bees make honey; and many people like to eat honey; Bees pollinate plants and that helps them to grow.

**Day 5** (page 173)

See Opinion Writing Rubric on page 202.

# ANSWER KEY *(cont.)*

## Week 33: In the Wind

**Day 1** (page 174)

Responses could vary, leading to a discussion of the power of wind and size/weight of objects. Use these categories as a guideline:

Check Marked Bubbles (light wind): bubbles, kite, leaf, paper, feather, balloon

Starred Bubbles (strong wind): car, boat, windmill, rock, marble, tree branches

**Day 2** (page 175)

<u>Wind cannot be seen, but it is easy to see what wind does.</u> ~~Sometimes the weather is sunny.~~ Wind makes things move. It takes different types of wind to move different objects. When you blow air out of your mouth, you are making a little wind. You can blow through a straw and make a feather move. ~~It is fun to find feathers birds have lost.~~ The harder you blow, the farther you can move it. Wind from a fan can make the feather move even further. You can see that it is windy outdoors when tree branches move. This kind of wind helps move kites up into the sky. ~~Kites have many colorful designs and are pretty to see.~~ On a windy day, you can see papers and leaves moving in the wind. <u>Even though you cannot see the wind, if you watch carefully, you know where it is.</u>

**Day 4** (page 177)

Words that should be crossed out:

1. heat, rain shower
2. rock, burn
3. horse, bike
4. radio, map

**Day 5** (page 178)

Yes; all the sentences are about wind.

## Week 34: Push or Pull

**Day 3** (page 181)

When you play tug-of-war, teams are pulling on opposite sides of a rope. Tug-of-war is a good example of using a strong force to pull.

When you walk and push a stroller, the stroller moves slowly. A stroller moves quickly if you are running while you push it.

When you shoot a basketball, you are pushing it. Soccer players push the ball as they kick it down the field.

If you are inside a car, you push the door to open it. If you are outside a car, you open the door by pulling on it.

**Day 4** (page 182)

1. If you walk slowly while pulling a wagon, ~~they~~ **(it)** will move slowly.
2. When you hit a baseball with a bat, you are really pushing ~~them~~ **(it)**.
3. The children pushed ~~his~~ **(their)** race cars down the track.
4. A boat moves when the wind pushes against ~~their~~ **(its)** sails.

**Day 5** (page 183)

See Informative/Explanatory Writing Rubric on page 203.

## Week 35: Watching TV or Reading?

**Day 2** (page 185)

It is fun to have free time, but deciding what to do can be difficult. I think it is better to spend free time reading books. ~~When you read books, you can learn.~~ ~~You can learn~~ about people, places, and animals all over the world. ~~You can learn~~ about how things grow and how things work. ~~When you read books, you can imagine.~~ ~~You can imagine~~ you are the character in the story and that you are experiencing the same things the character is. ~~When you read books, you get better~~ at reading. ~~You get better~~ at recognizing words, reading words correctly, and understanding new words. When you have free time, you really should choose to read a book.

**Day 4** (page 187)

Words that should be deleted:

1. Many people think that
2. Everyone should

## Week 36: Beach or Park?

**Day 4** (page 192)

1. I think the beach is the best place to go in the summer, ~~I think~~.
2. Everyone needs to spend time at the park ~~the park~~ to get exercise and have fun.
3. The best thing about going to the beach is getting ice cream on the way home, ~~that's the best thing~~.
4. The park near my house is the greatest ~~greatest~~ park of all.

**Day 5** (page 193)

See Opinion Writing Rubric on page 202.

# OPINION WRITING RUBRIC

**Directions:** Evaluate students' work in each category by circling one number in each row. Students have opportunities to score up to five points in each row and up to 15 points total.

| | Exceptional Writing | Quality Writing | Developing Writing |
|---|---|---|---|
| **Focus and Organization** | Clearly states an opinion that is relevant to the topic.<br><br>Demonstrates clear understanding of the intended audience and purpose of the piece.<br><br>Organizes ideas in a purposeful way and includes an introduction, a detailed body, and a conclusion. | States an opinion that is relevant to the topic.<br><br>Demonstrates some understanding of the intended audience and purpose of the piece.<br><br>Organizes ideas and includes an introduction, a body, and a conclusion. | States an unclear opinion that is not fully relevant to the topic.<br><br>Demonstrates little understanding of the intended audience or purpose of the piece.<br><br>Does not include an introduction, a body, or a conclusion. |
| **Points** | 5          4 | 3          2 | 1          0 |
| **Written Expression** | Uses descriptive and precise language with clarity and intention.<br><br>Maintains a consistent voice and uses an appropriate tone that supports meaning.<br><br>Uses multiple sentence types and transitions smoothly between ideas. | Uses a broad vocabulary.<br><br>Maintains a consistent voice and supports a tone and feeling through language.<br><br>Varies sentence length and word choices. | Uses a limited or an unvaried vocabulary.<br><br>Provides an inconsistent or a weak voice and tone.<br><br>Provides little to no variation in sentence type and length. |
| **Points** | 5          4 | 3          2 | 1          0 |
| **Language Conventions** | Capitalizes, punctuates, and spells accurately.<br><br>Demonstrates complete thoughts within sentences, with accurate subject-verb agreement.<br><br>Uses paragraphs appropriately and with clear purpose. | Capitalizes, punctuates, and spells accurately.<br><br>Demonstrates complete thoughts within sentences and appropriate grammar.<br><br>Paragraphs are properly divided and supported. | Incorrectly capitalizes, punctuates, and spells.<br><br>Uses fragmented or run-on sentences.<br><br>Utilizes poor grammar overall.<br><br>Paragraphs are poorly divided and developed. |
| **Points** | 5          4 | 3          2 | 1          0 |

**Total Points:** _____

# INFORMATIVE/EXPLANATORY WRITING RUBRIC

**Directions:** Evaluate students' work in each category by circling one number in each row. Students have opportunities to score up to five points in each row and up to 15 points total.

| | Exceptional Writing | Quality Writing | Developing Writing |
|---|---|---|---|
| **Focus and Organization** | Clearly states the topic and purposefully develops it throughout the writing.<br><br>Demonstrates clear understanding of the intended audience and purpose of the piece.<br><br>Organizes the information into a well-supported introduction, body, and conclusion. | States the topic and develops it throughout the writing.<br><br>Demonstrates some understanding of the intended audience and purpose of the piece.<br><br>Organizes the information into an introduction, body, and conclusion. | Does not state the topic and/or develop it throughout the writing.<br><br>Demonstrates little understanding of the intended audience or purpose of the piece.<br><br>Fails to organize the information into an introduction, body, or conclusion. |
| **Points** | 5      4 | 3      2 | 1      0 |
| **Written Expression** | Uses descriptive and precise language with clarity and intention.<br><br>Maintains a consistent voice and uses an appropriate tone that supports meaning.<br><br>Uses multiple sentence types and transitions smoothly between ideas. | Uses a broad vocabulary.<br><br>Maintains a consistent voice and supports a tone and feeling through language.<br><br>Varies sentence length and word choices. | Uses a limited or an unvaried vocabulary.<br><br>Provides an inconsistent or a weak voice and tone.<br><br>Provides little to no variation in sentence type and length. |
| **Points** | 5      4 | 3      2 | 1      0 |
| **Language Conventions** | Capitalizes, punctuates, and spells accurately.<br><br>Demonstrates complete thoughts within sentences, with accurate subject-verb agreement.<br><br>Uses paragraphs appropriately and with clear purpose. | Capitalizes, punctuates, and spells accurately.<br><br>Demonstrates complete thoughts within sentences and appropriate grammar.<br><br>Paragraphs are properly divided and supported. | Incorrectly capitalizes, punctuates, and spells.<br><br>Uses fragmented or run-on sentences.<br><br>Utilizes poor grammar overall.<br><br>Paragraphs are poorly divided and developed. |
| **Points** | 5      4 | 3      2 | 1      0 |

**Total Points:** _____

# NARRATIVE WRITING RUBRIC

**Directions:** Evaluate students' work in each category by circling one number in each row. Students have opportunities to score up to five points in each row and up to 15 points total.

|  | Exceptional Writing | Quality Writing | Developing Writing |
|---|---|---|---|
| **Focus and Organization** | Identifies the topic of the story and maintains the focus throughout the writing.<br><br>Develops clear settings, a strong plot, and interesting characters.<br><br>Demonstrates clear understanding of the intended audience and purpose of the piece.<br><br>Engages the reader from the opening hook through the middle to the conclusion. | Identifies the topic of the story, but has some trouble maintaining the focus throughout the writing.<br><br>Develops settings, a plot, and characters.<br><br>Demonstrates some understanding of the intended audience and purpose of the piece.<br><br>Includes an interesting opening, a strong story, and a conclusion. | Fails to identify the topic of the story or maintain focus throughout the writing.<br><br>Does not develop strong settings, plot, or characters.<br><br>Demonstrates little understanding of the intended audience or purpose of the piece.<br><br>Provides lack of clarity in the beginning, middle, and/or conclusion. |
| **Points** | 5          4 | 3          2 | 1          0 |
| **Written Expression** | Uses descriptive and precise language with clarity and intention.<br><br>Maintains a consistent voice and uses an appropriate tone that supports meaning.<br><br>Uses multiple sentence types and transitions smoothly between ideas. | Uses a broad vocabulary.<br><br>Maintains a consistent voice and supports a tone and feeling through language.<br><br>Varies sentence length and word choices. | Uses a limited or an unvaried vocabulary.<br><br>Provides an inconsistent or a weak voice and tone.<br><br>Provides little to no variation in sentence type and length. |
| **Points** | 5          4 | 3          2 | 1          0 |
| **Language Conventions** | Capitalizes, punctuates, and spells accurately.<br><br>Demonstrates complete thoughts within sentences, with accurate subject-verb agreement.<br><br>Uses paragraphs appropriately and with clear purpose. | Capitalizes, punctuates, and spells accurately.<br><br>Demonstrates complete thoughts within sentences and appropriate grammar.<br><br>Paragraphs are properly divided and supported. | Incorrectly capitalizes, punctuates, and spells.<br><br>Uses fragmented or run-on sentences.<br><br>Utilizes poor grammar overall.<br><br>Paragraphs are poorly divided and developed. |
| **Points** | 5          4 | 3          2 | 1          0 |

**Total Points:** _____

# OPINION WRITING ANALYSIS

**Directions:** Record each student's rubric scores (page 202) in the appropriate columns. Add the totals every two weeks and record the sums in the Total Scores column. You can view: (1) which students are not understanding the opinion genre and (2) how students progress after multiple encounters with the opinion genre.

| Student Name | Week 6 | Week 10 | Week 12 | Week 22 | Week 32 | Week 36 | Total Scores |
|---|---|---|---|---|---|---|---|
| | | | | | | | |
| | | | | | | | |
| | | | | | | | |
| | | | | | | | |
| | | | | | | | |
| | | | | | | | |
| | | | | | | | |
| | | | | | | | |
| | | | | | | | |
| | | | | | | | |
| | | | | | | | |
| | | | | | | | |
| | | | | | | | |
| | | | | | | | |
| | | | | | | | |
| **Average Classroom Score** | | | | | | | |

# INFORMATIVE/EXPLANATORY WRITING ANALYSIS

**Directions:** Record each student's rubric score (page 203) in the appropriate columns. Add the totals every two weeks and record the sums in the Total Scores column. You can view: (1) which students are not understanding the informative/explanatory genre and (2) how students progress after multiple encounters with the informative/explanatory genre.

| Student Name | Week 4 | Week 8 | Week 14 | Week 20 | Week 26 | Week 34 | Total Scores |
|---|---|---|---|---|---|---|---|
|  |  |  |  |  |  |  |  |
|  |  |  |  |  |  |  |  |
|  |  |  |  |  |  |  |  |
|  |  |  |  |  |  |  |  |
|  |  |  |  |  |  |  |  |
|  |  |  |  |  |  |  |  |
|  |  |  |  |  |  |  |  |
|  |  |  |  |  |  |  |  |
|  |  |  |  |  |  |  |  |
|  |  |  |  |  |  |  |  |
|  |  |  |  |  |  |  |  |
|  |  |  |  |  |  |  |  |
|  |  |  |  |  |  |  |  |
|  |  |  |  |  |  |  |  |
|  |  |  |  |  |  |  |  |
| **Average Classroom Score** |  |  |  |  |  |  |  |

# NARRATIVE WRITING ANALYSIS

**Directions:** Record each student's rubric score (page 204) in the appropriate columns. Add the totals every two weeks and record the sums in the Total Scores column. You can view: (1) which students are not understanding the narrative genre and (2) how students progress after multiple encounters with the narrative genre.

| Student Name | Week 2 | Week 16 | Week 18 | Week 24 | Week 28 | Week 30 | Total Scores |
|---|---|---|---|---|---|---|---|
| | | | | | | | |
| | | | | | | | |
| | | | | | | | |
| | | | | | | | |
| | | | | | | | |
| | | | | | | | |
| | | | | | | | |
| | | | | | | | |
| | | | | | | | |
| | | | | | | | |
| | | | | | | | |
| | | | | | | | |
| | | | | | | | |
| **Average Classroom Score** | | | | | | | |

# THE WRITING PROCESS

### STEP 1: PREWRITING

Think about the topic. Brainstorm ideas, and plan what you want to include in your writing.

### STEP 2: DRAFTING

Use your brainstormed ideas to write a first draft. Don't worry about errors. This will be a rough draft.

### STEP 3: REVISING

Read your rough draft. Think about the vocabulary you used and how your writing is organized. Then, make the appropriate changes to improve your written piece.

### STEP 4: EDITING

Reread your revised draft. Check for errors in spelling, punctuation, and grammar. Use editing marks to correct the errors.

### STEP 5: PUBLISHING

Create a final version of your piece, including the corrections from the edited version. Be sure to reread your work for any errors.

# EDITING MARKS

| Editing Marks | Symbol Names | Example |
|---|---|---|
| ≡ | capitalization symbol | <u>d</u>avid gobbled up the grapes.<br>≡ |
| / | lowercase symbol | My mother hugged /Me when I /Came /Home. |
| ⊙ | insert period symbol | The clouds danced in the sky⊙ |
| sp ◯ | check spelling symbol | I ⟨laffed⟩ at the story.<br>sp |
| ∿ | transpose symbol | How you are? |
| ∧ | insert symbol | Would you∧pass the pizza?<br>please |
| ∧̣ | insert comma symbol | I have two cats, two dogs∧and a goldfish.<br>, |
| ⌄ ⌄ | insert quotations symbol | ⌄That's amazing,⌄she shouted. |
| ℓ | deletion symbol | Will you call call me on the phone tonight? |
| ¶ | new paragraph symbol | … in the tree. ¶After lunch, I spent the day… |
| # | add space symbol | I ran to#the tree. |

# OPINION WRITING TIPS

## Ask yourself . . .                    ## Remember . . .

| Ask yourself . . . | Remember . . . |
|---|---|
| Do I have a strong belief in my opinion so that I can convince others to believe the same? | Make sure you can back up your opinion with specific examples. |
| Have I stated my opinion in a way that grabs the reader's attention? | Begin with a question or a bold statement that includes your opinion. |
| Do I have at least three reasons based on facts for my opinion? | Include at least three solid reasons why the reader should agree with you. |
| Do I have an example for each reason that strengthens my argument? | Each reason must be followed by one strong example. |
| Do I have a logical order to my writing? | Don't bounce around. Focus on a logical order to present each reason and example. |
| Am I using smooth transitions to connect my thoughts and help my writing flow? | Use transition words like *first, in addition to, another reason,* and *most important.* |
| Does my conclusion restate my opinion? | Do not forget to restate your opinion in the final sentence. |
| Have I used correct spelling, grammar, and punctuation? | Revisit what you have written. Then, check for mistakes. |

# INFORMATIVE/EXPLANATORY WRITING TIPS

## Ask yourself . . .

Do I provide enough information on the topic?

Have I narrowed the focus of the topic?

Does my writing have a hook?

Is my information presented in a logical order?

Have I included enough information that the reader will be interested in learning even more?

Have I used correct spelling, grammar, and punctuation?

## Remember . . .

Make sure to include facts about the topic in your writing so that the reader is informed.

Choose one aspect of the topic that you want to write about.

Begin with a strong topic sentence that grabs the reader's attention.

Do not bounce around. Present each topic sentence at the beginning of a paragraph and add details.

End with a strong sentence that makes the reader want to learn more about the subject.

Revisit what you have written. Then, check for mistakes.

# NARRATIVE WRITING TIPS

## Ask yourself . . .

## Remember . . .

Am I the main character? Is the story told from my point of view?

You are in the story, telling where you are, what you see, who you are with, and what you do.

Does my story have a hook?

Include an exciting introductory sentence that makes the reader want to continue reading.

Does my story make sense and have a beginning, a middle, and an end?

Do not bounce around. Focus on a logical order of how the experience happened.

Am I using transitions to connect my thoughts and help the writing flow?

Use transition words like *first, next, then, another,* and *finally.*

Am I including rich details and sensory language to help paint a picture in the reader's mind?

Use lots of adjectives, and incorporate figurative language, such as metaphors and similes, to make your story come to life.

Does my conclusion summarize the main idea?

Incorporate a sentence or two that reflects on what you have written.

Have I used correct spelling, grammar, and punctuation?

Revisit what you have written. Then, check for mistakes.

Opinion Writing

# Informative/Explanatory Writing

Narrative Writing

# DIGITAL RESOURCES

## Accessing the Digital Resources

The digital resources can be downloaded by following these steps:

**1.** Go to **www.tcmpub.com/digital**

**2.** Sign in or create an account.

**3.** Click **Redeem Content** and enter the ISBN number, located on page 2 and the back cover, into the appropriate field on the website.

**ISBN:**
**9781425815257**

**4.** Respond to the prompts using the book to view your account and available digital content.

**5.** Choose the digital resources you would like to download.  You can download all the files at once, or you can download a specific group of files.

**Please note:** Some files provided for download have large file sizes.  Download times for these larger files will vary based on your download speed.

---

 ## CONTENTS OF THE DIGITAL RESOURCES

### Teacher Resources

- Informative/Explanatory Writing Analysis
- Narrative Writing Analysis
- Opinion Writing Analysis
- Writing Rubric
- Writing Signs

### Student Resources

- Peer/Self-Editing Checklist
- Editing Marks
- Practice Pages
- The Writing Process
- Writing Prompts
- Writing Tips